That's W

- Thoughts on the P

L. D. Staudt

Illustrations by Will Guppy

ISBN 978-1-9161411-9-3

Foreword

Introduction

Most people are curious about the meaning and purpose of their lives, but few pursue it in any depth. There are a number of reasons for this:

- people are too busy
- people feel that the subject is too complicated, and leave it to the philosophers
- people reject the guidance from religion on the subject as simplistic, dogmatic, or nonsensical
- people have a fear of having to change their opinions and their ways
- people fear ridicule from friends and family

On that last point, if conversation amongst friends is lagging and you want to get a laugh, all you have to say is "Let's talk about the meaning of life." Sad, but often true. In general it is hard to have a serious discussion on the subject, yet it is obviously central to our lives. This book is a contribution to opening up this discussion.

First, here is some encouragement to those who feel they want to go down this road: whenever we try to increase our knowledge on any subject, we gain insights. You undoubtedly have had the experience of trying something new and then surprising yourself when you found that you eventually could do it. I remember my first physics course in university; I opened the text in the middle, looked at the formulas, and immediately closed the book. There was no way that stuff was ever going to make sense to me! However, I applied myself and by the time I got to the middle of the book I was beginning to understand the wonderful framework that physics provides for the physical world. Another example is when I started taking guitar lessons. I thought I would never be as good as my guitar teacher. But after two or three years I had to get more advanced instruction because I had reached the level of my first teacher.

So you can be absolutely confident that you can advance your understandings on this subject as well. It turns out that the basic concepts are not all that difficult, which is only fair since every human being should be able to understand what his or her life is about.

Even though we will necessarily discuss spiritual subjects, I will never ask you to abandon critical thinking. My hope for you is that by taking the time to think deeply about these things you will develop your own insights. Because it will take a few chapters before getting to the central idea of meaning and purpose in life, we will start with a summary chapter to give you an idea of where the book is going. Then we will go on to develop the points in the summary chapter in more detail. Here are some of the subjects discussed in this small book:

- the different levels of being (mineral, vegetable, animal, etc.)

- the existence of an ordering, intelligent Force
- life after this one
- how things have developed since the Big Bang
- where humanity has been and where it might be going
- the purpose and meaning of life, both general and specific to you
- our place in the natural world
- benefits that result from knowledge of purpose

Many people have thought about this question, and there is no shortage of academic treatises on the subject. My approach is more along the lines of engineering rather than science. This means that I will try to distil information to a level that is actually useful, rather than dwelling on details. In other words this book, while not being simple, will try to be more practical than many others.

I would also like to say that it is my firm conviction that humanity will successfully negotiate the present challenging times and achieve a maturity where the potentials of most human beings will be realized. This implies that in due course knowledge will advance at a pace we cannot imagine, which will make today's thinking seem elementary. However I do believe the book is topical and useful for the times we live in, and that many of the concepts expressed will stand the test of time.

Please note that I have tried to avoid the excessive use of references, with the exception of the essays in the Appendix. This should reduce distraction while reading. If you are interested in the sources of the quotations in the main chapters, it is easy enough to type the quotations into Google. Also note that these ideas are colored by the fact that I am a member of the Bahá'í Faith, the most recent of the world's great religions. However I have used concepts that are "generic" in a religious sense, which was not too hard given that they are all from the same source.

Finally, my sincere gratitude must be given to the contributors who assisted in the creation of this book: my wife Dawn for her constant encouragement and comments, Peter Oldziey and Earl Redman for their valuable review of the content, and to my son-in-law Will Guppy (willguppy@live.com) for his excellent and creative illustrations. Note that there is a series of video presentations on the book - search for Lawrence Staudt on YouTube and you will find them.

Lawrence Staudt
July 2023

Table of Contents

Chapter 1 – Summary and Overview

When I was young, I always hoped someone would tell me what my life was about, but no-one did. I came to understand that many people, without thinking about it very hard, thought life was simply about making more and more money and then retiring comfortably. This didn't seem like enough, but I carried on with this question mark over my life until I was out on my own. In my first full-time job, my immediate boss was nearing retirement age. He and I had attended the presentation of an engineering sales proposal that was solidly rejected by the intended client. As we left the meeting I commented on how poorly it had gone, and my boss gave me his wisdom, which included the statement "you have to learn to play the game." I took it to mean that he thought life was a game, with a mindless focus on "winning", whatever that meant. This seemed to be as far as his life philosophy went, and I decided that this was not going to be me in forty years. That was when I began to actively make investigations into what my life might be about.

Imagine that you are a boxer, and as you enter the ring you forget not only about the techniques of boxing but also about the fundamental rules of the sport. You wonder "What am I doing here?", and then of course you suffer greatly at the hands of your opponent. This is how life can seem to us; chaotic, painful, and meaningless, and then at the end you don't just get knocked out - you die! You learn to enjoy the rewarding moments of love and success, but you know that a new problem will soon arrive. Referring to these problems, the actor Tom Hanks once said "As far as I can tell it's just one thing after another." Murphy's Law seems to be a real thing.

People come to think about this subject for a variety of reasons, some of which are painful. For example, I have a friend whose pregnant wife was killed by a drunk driver. He was angry that God could allow such a thing to happen. He eventually learned to put that horrific tragedy into a general understanding of life, but at the time it was pure grief. We want and need to be able to put our lives into the context of a purpose, if such a thing can be found. We want to know what's it all about.

I am sure that many readers have had their own thoughts on this subject, based on their own life experiences. Please forgive me if this book comes across as being the only way to approach this subject – that is not my intention. However, I do hope this book can supplement your own ideas, and that you find it helpful.

The book tries to put this subject into some kind of logical framework – a framework for understanding life. While you can think as deeply as you like about the purpose of life and never stop gaining insights, the basics seem to be pretty simple, and in this first section I want to propose what I think are the basics. These ideas are developed further later in the book, but I didn't want you to have to wait several chapters before getting to the point. In the Appendices a couple of ideas are developed to a fairly deep level, just to show that there is really no end to such explorations. However, what I hope you will most seriously consider are the ideas in this first section - the basics.

The Basics

In most of the activities of life, it helps to learn the basics. The first thing is to have an understanding of what you are trying to achieve. Next you need to figure out how you are going to achieve it. Then you take steps to achieve it, and eventually (hopefully) you succeed. For example suppose you decide to become an electrician. You begin to pursue an education in this area, do an apprenticeship, and eventually achieve your goal. Life is a process as well - but what is our goal?

Along the way to achieving proficiency in any activity, we need to learn basic skills. As children playing our first baseball in the Little League we were taught to throw properly. If you were right-handed, the idea was to end up on your left foot as you released the ball. You would actually never be any good if you threw with your right hand while standing on your right foot. Also, when you were trying to hit the ball, you needed to have a level swing and not an uppercut. This would increase your chances of batting success.

We gradually gained intimate knowledge of the rules and strategies of the game. Many of these were learned through experience as opposed to formal teaching.

It was also useful to have some kind of philosophy of the game. In baseball we were taught that it doesn't matter if you win or lose - it's how you play the game. In other words trying your best and being a good sport were more important than winning. This was a useful (and correct) perspective, which helped greatly when we lost a game.

Without basic skills, we would not have been good baseball players. That overarching philosophy allowed us to put a bigger framework around the simple game of baseball. The philosophy outlasted my baseball career, being useful in life in general. It taught us to strive for excellence but to accept setbacks gracefully, a very useful skill since there are many setbacks in life and you need to be comfortable with them.

So what we are proposing is that it would be useful to know the basic goals, rules, and skills of life itself. With this knowledge we might be able to understand and better cope with the events of our lives.

So what is the objective of your life? Are your trying to "win", and if so what do you consider "winning" to be?

We live in a materialistic society, and so naturally enough we tend to measure our success in those terms. Do we have enough to go on a holiday each year? Can we afford the fees to give our children a good education? Can I enjoy a night out at the pub without pinching pennies? Will I have enough for a comfortable retirement? But we also think about other things that are less easy to measure. We want to be happy. We want to have fewer troubles. We want to be content.

In order to consider these questions and the more general question of purpose, we need to have some kind of framework for understanding life. That is what the first part of the book is about.

Levels of Existence

The first question addressed in Chapter 2 is where we, as human beings, fit into the world around us. As we observe nature, we see that there are different levels of complexity. The mineral level has some kind of physical structure. For example a diamond is a beautiful and regular arrangement of carbon atoms. Next is the vegetable level which, besides structure, has the added power of life. For example a rose is a beautiful arrangement of atoms, but it is also alive - growing and reproducing.

Next we have the animal level, which has physical structure and life, but has the added feature of consciousness. After that we have the human level, which embodies the characteristic of all previous levels but with added features such as the capabilities of abstract thought and free will. For better or for worse, we have the ability to act outside of the laws of nature.

Besides being an interesting lens through which we can think of the world, it also begs the question: Are there levels above us? The book gives logical arguments for the existence of levels above us, which we cannot fully understand and to which we cannot aspire (in the same way a cow cannot understand or aspire to be a mathematician).

On that basis we then argue for the existence of an unknowable creator. The existence of a creation means there must be a creator in the same way that if you see a painting, you know for a fact that there is a painter. For many of us these things go without saying, but others need more persuasive logic for believing in a creative force in the universe, and we develop these thoughts in some detail in Chapter 2.

We also briefly discuss the idea of a life of some sort after this life. Of course this idea has been taught by all the great religions, but it is rather hard to verify! However, there are multiple accounts of near-death experiences, most of which have common features; watching the your body from nearby, moving toward a light, being met by a caring being, reviewing your life on earth, etc.

The analogy can be made with a child in the womb. It has no notion of what is coming next. It occasionally gets hints of something from its next life, such as music and voices. Yet a vast world awaits, along with a host of caring people that can't wait to greet it. We see that this is clearly the case in this life, and the hope is that a similar experience awaits us when we move on to some sort of life after this one.

We won't know the reality of the next life until we get there, but in Chapter 2 we develop the idea that it will probably be a positive experience. Also, it seems clear that we don't take anything with us into the next life ("you can't take it with you") – we only take our spirit or soul. All of this background information helps put a perspective on our purpose in life when we get to Chapter 4. But first more background information is presented in Chapter 3.

Human Development

Chapter 3 starts with the Big Bang, and goes on to discuss how it is unlikely that an ordered universe could result from an explosion. The complexity of cells is discussed, and the unlikely coming into being of the first cell. Nonetheless this happened, and then life just couldn't be stopped.

We then discuss how consciousness miraculously appeared as the first animals came into being, and we then had an entire world operating according to the laws of nature, including our ancestors who were happily engaged in living the animal life. But somehow we began operating outside of the laws of nature, and then the trouble really began. The planet began to suffer from our misbehavior. This is when human beings, complete with free will and the capability of abstract thought, became separate from the animal level of being.

Then we began to develop socially, with more and more complex levels of organization. We started living as families, then groups of families in a village, then groups of villages in a kingdom, then groups of kingdoms became nations. This took place over the course of millennia. It is proposed that the natural next step for us is an additional layer of organization at the world level. Chapter 3 also discusses spiritual development, which in general took place under the guidance of religious systems.

Purpose

Chapter 4 is the core of the book, developing concepts related to human purpose, based on the previous chapters. Suppose you are out shopping, and you come across an appliance called an air fryer. You have never seen one before and you don't know what it is. So you read on the box what the manufacturer has to say about it, and you begin to understand its purpose. The manufacturer is intimately acquainted with the air fryer, from the microprocessor that controls it, to the thermal design that properly cooks the food, and a myriad other details. But you are only given information in the user manual that is useful to you, and that you can understand. Of course you may be one of those that does not read the instructions at all...

The point is: the purpose of the creation (air fryer) is known by its creator. It is also obvious that the creator is superior to the creation. The creator is an engineer who has life and consciousness, whereas the air fryer has neither. It is proposed that this is the case with our creator compared to us. For example our creator knows everything, since he made everything (or, maybe more accurately, the process that resulted in everything). We see that our creator is on a level above us that we can only have a limited understanding of. Logical and humility-inducing!

Knowledge of the created thing is known by its creator, so it is proposed we should look in the direction of our creator if we want to know our purpose. Where do we find out what our creator has to say? It is proposed that our creator has given guidance in the form of religion ever since we evolved to a state that we could take it on board. The guidance comes in the same way every time: a humble soul is born who brings a message that eventually transforms individuals and societies for the better, a message that somehow prevails even though the messenger has no status, education, or material means. It is a very unlikely event with nonetheless is periodically repeated throughout human history, and only in religion.

If this is true, then it makes sense to explore what these messengers had to say about the purpose of your life. As you would expect, their messages are similar, since they are from the same source (with the exception of some social teachings, which were specific to time and place). So now to the heart of the matter:

It is proposed that **this life serves the purpose of developing our souls in preparation for existence in the next life.** We only take our souls with us when we die, and just like a child in the womb our soul needs to be fully developed when we are born into whatever comes next. Our degree of development primarily depends on our efforts to become "good people" in this life. What constitutes a good person is laid out in the guidance in religion. So what we should be doing is finding out what the creator has to say about becoming a good person and then trying to implement it. This is the equivalent of actually reading the air fryer instruction manual. It is a good idea.

But it is sometimes not easy to determine what religion really has to say, since over time many of the pure teachings have been overlaid with man-made interpretations and dogma. This is probably the main reason for a perceived conflict between science and religion - the idea that we need to abandon critical thinking when we consider religion. New science has rejected old religion, and as a result many people have rejected religion altogether, and wouldn't even consider seeking guidance from religion. If you have come to this conclusion, please reconsider, realizing that what your idea of religion or God is can possibly be understood in a different way. This is considered later in the book and in Appendix 3.

In the past, religion was brought to the illiterate masses through the necessary intermediary of an educated priesthood. However, we are now (it is proposed) approaching maturity as a race, and one of the characteristics of human maturity is independent thinking. We can now make our own investigations of spiritual matters and discover many interesting things, including knowledge of purpose.

There is a second aspect to life purpose, and that is this: we are all unique individuals, with unique talents and capacities. It is proposed (and religion tells us) that **the second aspect of our purpose is to develop our particular talents and capacities in order to subsequently be of service to humanity.**

Our children seemed to have an intuitive idea of what they should do with their lives. The eldest was clear from a young age that his future had to do with computers, and now he works with Microsoft. The next was always attracted to working with children, and she now works with autistic children. The next was attracted to social service, and now works as a social worker. Finally, the fourth was our artist, who worked as a professional actor in London.

It seems we are attracted to particular careers or ways of being useful as adults. But whatever we do, we should be trying to be of service (see Appendix 1). This will have obvious benefits for those around us, while at the same time helping to develop ourselves spiritually.

Attitudes and Understandings

With this perspective, we then move on in Chapters 5 and 6 to discuss the natural result of this understanding of life and its purpose on human society moving forward. If we realize our basic purpose on this earth is spiritual development, then we can easily see that presently society is unbalanced. We are focused primarily on the material aspects of life. As we seek to balance the material and the spiritual, our lifestyles will become more moderate, and we will become happier and less worried. While advancing materially will continue to be important, we will begin to measure the "success" of our lives based on our spiritual development, since this is what benefits us in the long run. This is a mature and reasonable point of view, based on knowledge of purpose.

Our appreciation of the natural world will be enhanced, and we will better understand the need to live sustainably and preserve the planet so that future generations can develop here before they also move on. In other words we will become more responsible stewards of the planet, for a reason that transcends mere survival (though of course that's nice too).

Knowledge of purpose, both individually and collectively, will over the next few centuries play an important role in developing, for the first and only time, a peaceful global civilization. It is proposed that the human race will make it through the present period of chaotic adolescence and achieve a society where the organic oneness of the human race will be understood by all.

Chapter 2 - The World Around Us

Chapters 2 and 3 develop concepts that will be used subsequently in Chapter 4 where we discuss purpose and meaning in life.

Levels of Being

Imagine a farmer, leaning on a fence and gazing into a pasture. It is a field that is not particularly suitable for crops, since there are plenty of rocks. Imagine the fields of northern New England or western Ireland, which seem to grow rocks.

So first of all the farmer sees the rocks, then he sees the grass and maybe a tree, then he sees his prize bull. Let us consider these four "levels of being." The rocks are composed of atoms, and have a structure or composition. The grass and the tree also have composition, but they also have an added quality which we'll call life. The bull not only has composition and life, but also has sense perception and consciousness. Finally we look at the farmer, who has the first three qualities plus the capability of abstract thought. Also, he is also not "hardwired" to the laws of Nature. For example, bees are hardwired to make their honeycomb in the shape of a hexagon - they never consider other options. The farmer is not similarly constrained - he has free will and has the option of not obeying the laws of nature. So it appears there are different "levels of being." We can represent this as follows:

Level of Being	Composition?	Life?	Consciousness?	Abstract Thought?
Mineral	✓	X	X	X
Vegetable	✓	✓	X	X
Animal	✓	✓	✓	X
Human	✓	✓	✓	✓

There is an excellent treatment of this concept of levels of being in E. F. Schumacher's book "A Guide for the Perplexed." Besides recognizing and describing these levels, a pertinent additional point Schumacher makes is that science has never actually explained life, consciousness, or our capability of abstract thought. These three represent the sudden jumps (discontinuities) between the levels which distinguish them from each other. Schumacher makes the point that while the *existence* of these discontinuities or jumps is recognized in science, science does not explain what they *are*, and cannot infuse life or consciousness into things that aren't alive.

Life

Science does precisely explain what a diamond (part of the mineral level) *is* - it is a particular arrangement of carbon atoms. We can make a synthetic diamond thanks to our understanding of its atomic structure. In fact we can now construct various things atom by atom (though it is very time consuming, as you can imagine).

However, science has not been able to synthesize life. We cannot even find some kind of life force under the microscope, though we can obviously see when something is alive (i.e. when it *has* a life force). The same is true of consciousness as well as the capability of abstract thought. The point we are making is that these discontinuities are clearly beyond human understanding, other than knowing they exist. This leads to the question as to how these things came into being, which we will discuss later.

Let us discuss the life discontinuity further. Our planet formed about 4.5 billion years ago and life appeared a mere 700 million years later. So 3.8 billion years ago there was a very important event in the history of the planet - the appearance of life. In Bill Bryson's "A Short History of Nearly Everything", he discusses an attempt of science to synthesize life:

> "In 1953 Stanley Miller, a graduate student at the University of Chicago, took two flasks - one containing a little water to represent a primeval ocean, the other holding a mixture of methane, ammonia and hydrogen sulfide gases to represent the Earth's early atmosphere - connected them with rubber tubes and introduced some electric sparks as a stand-in for lightning. After a few days, the water in the flasks had turned green and yellow in a hearty broth of amino acids, fatty acids, sugars and other organic compounds. 'If God didn't do it this way,' observed Miller's delighted supervisor, the Nobel laureate Harold Urey, 'He missed a good bet.'
>
> "Press reports of the time made it sound as if about all that was needed now was for somebody to give the flasks a good shake and life would crawl out. As time has shown, it wasn't nearly so simple. Despite half a century of further study, we are no

> nearer to synthesizing life today than we were in 1953 - and much further away from thinking we can."

Amino acids are called the building blocks of life, and primitive amino acids have indeed been synthesized in the lab. But as Bryson says:

> "At all events, creating amino acids is not really the problem. The problem is proteins. Proteins are what you get when you string amino acids together, and we need a lot of them. No-one really knows, but there may be as many as a million types of protein in the human body, and each one is a little miracle. By all the laws of probability proteins shouldn't exist."

He then discusses the formation of the human protein collagen:

> "To make collagen, you need to arrange 1,055 amino acids in precisely the right sequence. But - and here's an obvious but crucial point - *you* don't make it. It makes itself, spontaneously, without direction, and this is where the unlikelihoods come in.
>
> "The chances of a 1,055-sequence molecule like collagen spontaneously self-assembling are, frankly, nil. It just isn't going to happen. To grasp what a long shot its existence is, visualize a standard Las Vegas slot machine but broadened greatly - to about 27 meters, to be precise - to accommodate 1,055 spinning wheels instead of the usual three or four, and with twenty symbols

> on each wheel (one for each common amino acid). How long would you have to pull the handle before all 1,055 symbols came up in the right order? Effectively forever."

He goes on to say that even if you reduced the spinning wheels from 1,055 to 200 (a not unreasonable number of amino acids for other proteins), the odds of getting the correct sequence are about 1 in 10^{260} (1 followed by 260 zeros). That is a larger number than the number of atoms in the universe. So the odds of randomly producing the requisite proteins for life once you have the amino acids are vanishingly small, and *then* there is the challenge of somehow infusing them with "life." Bryson makes an analogy:

> "It is as if all the ingredients in your kitchen somehow got together and baked themselves into a cake - but a cake that could moreover divide when necessary to produce *more* cakes. It is little wonder that we call it the miracle of life. It is also little wonder that we have barely begun to understand it."

When we understand the complexity of the living cell, things become even more amazing. Bryson also tells us:

> "Every cell in nature is a thing of wonder. Even the simplest are far beyond the limits of human ingenuity. To build the most basic yeast cell, for example, you would have to miniaturize about the same number of components as are found in a Boeing 777 jetliner and fit them into a sphere just

> 5 microns across; then somehow you would have to persuade that sphere to reproduce." He goes on to say "If you could visit a (human) cell, you wouldn't like it. Blown up to a scale at which atoms were about the size of peas, a cell itself would be a sphere roughly half a mile across... Within it, millions upon millions of objects - some the size of basketballs, others the size of cars - would whiz about like bullets. There wouldn't be a place you could stand without being pummeled and ripped thousands of times every second from every direction....The proteins are especially lively, spinning, pulsating and flying into each other up to a billion times a second... all lead existences that are inconceivably frenzied."

Bryson gives many more interesting details, then quotes a scientist who said "the molecular world must necessarily remain entirely beyond the powers of our imagination owing to the incredible speed with which things happen in it." Science had no idea of these complexities in the 1950s.

This type of complex activity must have occurred in the first living cells. The proposal that it could have just "started happening" is obviously very unlikely. These understandings of the cell did not exist in the time of Darwin, and so these early understandings of evolution were naturally flawed and simplistic.

We have not only been unable to synthesize life from inanimate matter, we do not understand the science that makes life life. This supports Schumacher's point that science has never actually explained how life came into existence, never mind the yet more difficult questions of how consciousness and abstract thought came to be and what they actually are. The odds of them randomly appearing are vanishingly small.

Yet we are being asked by some scientists to believe that life *randomly* appeared in the universe, i.e. it was an accident. It takes more faith to believe this is true than to postulate the existence of some sort of creative force, i.e. the latter is far more probable than the former.

We therefore conclude that there is a superior intelligence behind all of this. As Einstein said: "My religion consists of a humble admiration of the illimitable superior spirit who reveals himself in the slight details we are able to perceive with our frail and feeble mind."

Other Levels of Being?

Now let us consider these levels of being further. We propose that "lower" levels, no matter how beautiful they may be, can never reach the next level. Quartz crystals cannot and will not, over time, become a flower - they will not acquire life. Cows cannot aspire to learn advanced mathematics. Of course the lower levels don't think about such things - they have no capability of abstract thought, remember? But as human beings we do think about such things, and it is important to be humble enough and wise enough to know the limitations of our own level (like Einstein).

Consider the farm scenario again. The tree dominates the soil in the sense that it thrusts its roots down and can even break rocks in the process. So the vegetable kingdom dominates the mineral kingdom. In the same way the animal level dominates the vegetable level. The bull eats the grass as it pleases, and the grass must submit. The farmer (human level) dominates over the bull (animal level), and in fact has the power of life and death over the bull. The bull is not aware of this fact. It is easy to imagine the farmer working in the field one day. The bull notices this, and chases the farmer out of "his" field. The bull has no comprehension of what it is to be human, and is simply dealing with the farmer as it would deal with another animal.

Is it not reasonable, then, that there could be levels of being above *us* that *we* cannot comprehend or appreciate? This must be accepted as a possibility - a humbling yet logical thought. We will return to this later.

The Existence of a Creative Force in the Universe

From the above, it appears there is a creative intelligence in the universe. There is an interesting discussion going on now between scientists who call themselves "scientific atheists" and the scientists who subscribe to the theory of "intelligent design." Scientific arguments are put forward by both parties regarding the existence of a creator. Scientific atheists are clear they cannot explain (or replicate) the emergence of life based on known science, but are hopeful this will eventually be understood. The scientists who see an intelligent designer behind the universe (per Einstein) point out that all living things have DNA in their cells, the "genetic code" that determines the features of an organism. Bill

Gates likens this to a computer programme. But a programme requires a programmer. This means the genetic code is a sure indicator of the intelligent entity behind it. In order for the first life to come into existence, it required a genetic code. But this could not have evolved out of nothing - this "programme" required a programmer before it came into existence. The intelligent design argument is gaining ground - and for a number seemingly irrefutable scientific reasons such as this.*

When discussing the existence of a creator with atheist friends, one of my standard lines is "The God you don't believe in? - I don't believe in it either." People often imagine what God is, and then announce they don't believe in such a creator. However, we must accept the principle that if we see a creation (e.g. a painting), then we can confidently predict that a creator (painter) exists. We are not yet talking about the nature of that creator, just that a creator must exist.

Here is a story to illustrate the point. There were two good friends - one (friend A) believed in God and the other (friend B) did not. They would get together for a cup of tea every week and enjoy each other's company, and one or the other friend would host the meeting. One week it was friend A's turn to host. For a few days before the meeting she was out in the workshop, working on a model of the solar system. It was a clever model of all the planets revolving around the sun,

---

* For example, see *The Return of the God Hypothesis* by Stephen Meyer (2021)

connected with little chains and pulleys, all driven by a little electric motor.

When the day came she put the model on the coffee table and plugged it in. She was out in the kitchen preparing the tea when the doorbell rang. Friend B let himself in and headed into the living room, immediately noticing the solar system model.

> Friend B: Wow - where did this come from?
> Friend A (calling in from the kitchen): What are you talking about?
> Friend B: Here, on the coffee table!
> Friend A (coming in with the tea): Well look at that.
> Friend B: Where did it come from?
> Friend A: I don't know. I guess it just appeared.
> Friend B: Just *appeared*? *Somebody* must have made it. Was it you?
> Friend A: Yes. I guess it has a creator...

Therefore we conclude that it is highly likely that our universe has a creator, since a creation proves the existence of a creator.

The Role of Religion

The idea of the existence of levels of being above the human level is a bit humbling, and a bit problematic. Since each level cannot understand the level above it, how are we to understand levels above us? The short answer is: we have been told about higher levels of existence via all the world's great religions, i.e. our creator has told us about these things, in such a way that we can have at least some idea about them.

This will be elaborated upon below, but first let us discuss the idea of religion. We have established the likelihood of there being a creator. It is clear that the creator is superior to the creation. For example, the painting tells us in some ways of the painter, but by no means is it a complete representation - the painter is much more. The painter is superior to the painting.

As mentioned, scientific atheists seem to jump through a lot of intellectual hoops in order to suggest that a creator need not exist. Their arguments are so complex that the average person cannot easily follow them. However, the knowledge that a creation proves the existence of some sort of creator doesn't require a PhD. For example, this has been known by native cultures for a long time. Part of our confusion arises from the fact that "new science" is debating the issue with "old religion." We might say that new science began with the advent of the scientific method (an ordered way of investigating natural phenomena - see Appendix 3), as first practiced by Galileo around 1600. Meanwhile old religion developed before then, and now contains many unreasonable man-made ideas. Many of the new scientists have quite rightly rejected that form of religion, but in the process have also rejected the idea of a creator, which turns out to be unscientific. It is more of a reaction to old religion, combined with the youthful enthusiasm of science that wants to believe that we can eventually understand everything, which is not possible for our level of being..

It is important for us to know as human beings that our ability to understand is limited compared to levels above us (per Einstein above). If you imagine the levels of being as shelves of infinite length and width, and that you can roam anywhere on the shelf. As human beings we can make infinite progress in any direction on the shelf. However, we will never move up to a higher shelf, or level of being, as discussed above. Therefore it is actually impossible for us to completely understand some things, and we should not reject certain ideas just because we cannot understand them.

It is proposed that our creator has indeed communicated with us and continues to do so via religion. Religion has been defined as "the revelation of the will of God." I propose the following, which is supported by history: periodically (every 1,000 years or so) a great religion appears. Society is transformed for the better over the next number of centuries as the religion brings its influence. This positive influence subsequently declines as the pure teachings are polluted by man-made dogma, and then this process repeats. So all of humanity has always had some level of guidance from the creator, given in this way. It is a repeatable, documented process, although it has suffered from human intervention.

Unfortunately, today religion is at a low ebb, and can be dismissed as illogical (which is often true) and irrelevant (which it is not – I would propose that the "baby has been thrown out with the bathwater"). Religion as defined above is not irrelevant, and it is proposed that it remains a necessary feature of human society. For example, it provides us with common standards. So as we move through the rest of this book, I will continue to use logic in discussing the purpose and meaning of our lives but I will also refer to religious teachings, i.e. what the creator has to say. We will keep in mind that there is only one creator, and therefore in a sense there is only one religion, brought to humanity at different places and times. Hence we find their messages are very similar, like different classes in the same school. If this is true, then it follows that they are fundamentally not in competition with each other, any more than third grade is in competition with second grade.

Let's go back to our farmer, who has just been chased out of his field by the ignorant bull. Imagine someone now walking up to him, a special someone with a peaceful glow about him. The farmer (who is a bit flustered) chases him away, regarding him as nothing but a trespasser. Little does the farmer know that this person, although in a human body, is actually "superhuman", i.e. a level of being above us (which we have already discussed as a logical possibility).

I propose that God has periodically sent these superhuman messengers (Buddha, Krishna, Moses, Christ, Muhammad, Bahá'u'lláh, etc.) to bring us information via the great religions. They are persecuted while in this life (getting chased off a farm pales in comparison to what each one of them has suffered), but a proof that they are superhuman is this: against all odds and with no worldly means (money, political sway, etc.) their message prevails and influences society for centuries to come. Strangely, this only happens in religion – a repeatable process in human history. This theory is in agreement with observed evidence. This is all to say that religious teachings should be included in our search for meaning in life.

Life After This Life

When a child is in the mother's womb, it is in the perfect situation to develop physically. All that it needs to prepare for its "next life" is provided, and when the time comes the child is born. The child when in the womb is almost entirely ignorant of what is coming next. It might pick up bits of sound such as music and speech (I used to talk to my unborn kids through my wife's tummy - who knows what the baby thought of that!). Even if you could communicate with the child, it could never understand what a tree is, or the sun. So the child remains ignorant of its next life until it gets there. The same is true of us. Even though some form of words has been used in religion and in books to describe near-death experiences, we really won't understand the next life until we get there. Religion tells us "the world beyond is as different from this world as this world is different from that of the child while still in the womb of its mother."

Religion also tells us that the next life is a good place ("heaven" or "nirvana"), and uses analogies to encourage us to develop ourselves for life after death. But for the reason above it actually cannot tell us exactly what the next life is like, because we wouldn't be able to understand it while still in this womb-world. People who return from near-death experiences find the next life very hard to explain.

There are various books about near-death experiences (NDEs), and although this evidence must be treated as anecdotal, there is certainly a lot of it. There is a particularly compelling book called *Proof of Heaven: A Neurosurgeon's Journey into the Afterlife* by Eben Alexander. Alexander is an eminent brain surgeon, who, after having had his near-death experience, reviews the medical data. He concluded that it was impossible that his experience was the last gasp of a dying organ, mostly since there was no brain activity at all during his NDE. He was not a religious man, but could only conclude that there is indeed an afterlife.

We were with my mother during her last days. She died peacefully in her sleep and was mentally aware and coherent during most of that time. On several occasions she saw old friends who had already passed on. She was a pragmatic woman with a good sense of humor. One time she told me "I just saw Bill Demers, but that's crazy"! But you could tell from her smile that she felt this was meaningful. I suggested to her that maybe she was not unlike a chick in the egg. Her egg was beginning to crack open and she could see bits of the world beyond.

We used to joke about who might be on the greeting committee when she arrived in the next life (besides Bill Demers). There seem to be various things that hint of the next life in this life, and it may be that birth into this life is like birth into the next life in the sense that you are greeted by people who love you and know you are coming. Religion tells us:

> "As to the question whether the souls will recognize each other in the spiritual world: This (fact) is certain; for the Kingdom is the world of vision, where all the concealed realities will become disclosed... The mysteries of which man is heedless in this earthly world, those will he discover in the heavenly world, and there will he be informed of the secret of truth; how much more will he recognize or discover persons with whom he hath been associated."

One of the more famous books concerning near-death experiences is Raymond Moody's *Life After Life*. The following incidents are taken from this book.

> "I realized that all these people were there, almost in multitudes it seems, hovering around the ceiling of the room. They were all people I had known in my past life, but who had passed on before. I recognized my grandmother and a girl I had known when I was in school, and many other relatives and friends. It seems that I mainly saw their faces and felt their presence. They all seemed pleased. It was a very happy occasion, and I felt that they had come to protect or to guide me .... It was a beautiful and glorious moment."

> "Several weeks before I nearly died, a good friend of mine, Bob, had been killed. Now the moment I got out of my body I had the feeling that Bob was standing there, right next to me. I could see him in my mind and felt like he was there, but it was strange. I didn't see him as his physical body

> ... He was there but he didn't have a physical body."
>
> "I had the feeling that there were people around me, and I could feel their presence, and could feel them moving, though I could never see anyone. Every now and then, I would talk with one of them, but I couldn't see them. And whenever I wondered what was going on, I would always get a thought back from one of them, that everything was all right, that I was dying but would be fine."

Any of the books on near-death experiences have been subject to some amount of criticism, and clearly those who want to continue to believe that this life is the only life can continue to do so, since as mentioned above the evidence is anecdotal and not definitive. However, this anecdotal evidence does match up pretty well with the information from our creator (i.e. religion), so I hope at this stage you agree there is a good possibility that there is a life after this one. Most people feel this is the case, but it never hurts to re-examine your thoughts on the subject.

So in this chapter we have established:

a) **There are different "levels of being" in the world around us (mineral, plant, animal, human)**
b) **We have a limited understanding of the properties which separate the different levels of being (life, consciousness, and the capacity for abstract thinking) and cannot replicate them**
c) **It is logical that there could be levels of being above us that we cannot comprehend or appreciate**

d) **The most probable explanation for creation is a creator, the author of the universe**
e) **The purpose of any creation is known by its creator**
f) **Religion is a repeatable phenomenon in human history, and seems to include information from our creator**
g) **Religious teachings should be considered in our quest for meaning in life**
h) **It is likely that we go on in some fashion after we die, to places we can only dimly visualize in this life**

These understandings, when combined with knowledge of purpose (Chapter 4), have major implications for how we treat the planet (Chapter 5) and live our lives (Chapter 6). But first let us consider how we (the human race) got to where we are.

Chapter 3 - Tracing Human Development

In Chapter 2 we developed a framework for understanding the world around us. In this chapter we present more background information regarding how humans and human society evolved to what we see now.

The Big Bang

So let's start with the Big Bang. First there was an explosion, as described by Bill Bryson in his *Short History of Nearly Everything*:

> "In a single blinding pulse, a moment of glory much too swift and expansive for any form of words, the singularity assumes heavenly dimensions, space beyond conception. The first lively second (a second that many cosmologists will devote careers to shaving into ever-finer wafers) produces gravity and the other forces that govern physics. In less than a minute the universe is a million billion miles across and growing fast. There is a lot of heat now, 10 billion degrees of it, enough to begin the nuclear reactions that create the lighter elements - principally hydrogen and helium, with a dash (about one atom in a hundred million) of lithium. In three minutes, 98 per cent of all matter there is or will ever be has been produced. We have a universe. It is a place of the most wondrous and gratifying possibility, and beautiful, too. And it was all done in about the time it takes to make a sandwich."

This is what science says, and it sounds like the universe had a beginning. Yet in religion the eternal nature of the universe is sometimes discussed, for example:

> "...God hath everlastingly existed, and will everlastingly continue to exist. His creation, likewise, hath had no beginning, and will have no end."

But religion also says there was a beginning: "In the beginning God created the heavens and the earth..."

When the physicist Dr Neil Turok was growing up in South Africa, one of his favorite teachers was a Scottish woman who told him "There is only one question that really matters: What banged?". This obviously made an impression on Dr Turok, because later in his life he became a leading cosmologist (physicist studying the early beginnings of the universe). Among other things he has investigated a cyclical model of the universe. This means there was a big bang, followed by a "big crunch", when gravity draws the universe back in on itself until it is all compressed into the singularity mentioned above, at which point there is another big bang and the process repeats. This theory is being debated in physics and may or may not gain universal (!) acceptance.

So we see that physics is also considering that while the present universe had a big bang beginning, the universe may also be cyclic, i.e. eternal. Both points of view may be accommodated by both science and religion. In fact new thinking demonstrates that there is no intrinsic conflict between science and religion - they are both aspects of truth. To quote Dr William Hatcher "A notable feature of the religion-science controversy as it has actually existed in our recent history is this: new science came into conflict with old religion." As previously discussed, many of the explanations and interpretations of religion were developed before "science" existed. In fact only one of the great religions appeared after the advent of the scientific method. Prior to that there was no attempt to put things in terms that agreed with science, since there was very little science and the vast majority of people were illiterate. So the old, dogmatic and often incorrect interpretations of religion are today compared with science and found to be unreasonable.

In fact there is no contradiction between true religion and science. When a religion is opposed to science it becomes mere superstition. That which is contrary to knowledge is ignorance. How can a man believe to be a fact that which science has proved to be impossible? If he believes in spite of his reason, it is likely to be ignorant superstition rather than faith. We propose that the true principles of all religions are in conformity with the teachings of science.

Of course the findings of science change over time. For example, Newtonian physics was felt to be an accurate way to model the physical world for more than a century. Then Einstein came along with the idea of relativity and showed that Newton's ideas were incomplete. So things that were "proven" by Newtonian physics were in question. The whole area of science vs religion is an idea worthy of investigation, and is discussed in Appendix 3.

So there was a Big Bang, i.e. an explosion. After a few billion years the result was the ordered universe as we know it. The key word here is "ordered". Since when does an explosion produce order? When something is blown up, it disintegrates, often turning to dust. But in this case the universe went from dust (atoms) to all kinds of ordered things. Not only ordered, but sometimes possessing life, consciousness, and the capacity for abstract thought. Wow.

It is common sense that, for example, a hurricane can take a brick house and reduce it to a pile of bricks. But in the case of the big bang the opposite seems to have occurred - in effect the hurricane produced a brick house (creation) from a pile of bricks (atoms).

Order vs Chaos

One of the fundamental laws in physics is the Second Law of Thermodynamics, which tells us that order is improbable - that things tend toward disorder. Anyone with children knows that this is true! So science tells us that the universe is very, very unlikely, since against all the odds it is ordered. We know that if order exists, then there must be an ordering force (see the above example of friend A and friend B). As mentioned earlier, the fact that there must be a creator has been obvious to human beings for millennia. It is only recently that some scientists have suggested that we don't need a creator - either that evolution and survival of the fittest has somehow resulted in greater order (discussed below), or that there are so many universes that one of them is bound to be ordered. This "multiverse" theory is increasingly discredited as being unscientific, especially since it cannot be tested - a fundamental requirement for the acceptance of any scientific theory.

The methods of calculating the probability of chance events have been well known in mathematics for many years. Dr Cyrus Varan tells us:

> "A full appreciation of the beauty of nature's order can best be realized by comprehending the limitations of chance events... A valuable measure of the limitations of chance events is provided by the prominent Canadian physicist, George Gamow. Gamow is credited with confirming the mathematical probability of the chance formation of a line of a book. For the proper positioning 50 letters, numbers and punctuation in an average of 65 spaces, Gamow confirmed that the coincidental probability is 1 against 10 to the power of 110 (i.e. one followed by 110 zeros). The age of the universe in seconds is less than 10 to the power of 18. On this basis, if there were a billion permutations in every second, then the time required to get 50 characters properly ordered in a line of a book by chance events is more than 10 to the power of 80 times the age of the universe... Thus, the chances against the random creation of an ordered line in a piece of written literature are incredibly immense."

Note that this seems to contradict the common proposition that if you had enough monkeys in front of typewriters, one of them would eventually produce the complete works of Shakespeare.

Earlier we gave Bryson's example of the vanishingly small probability of a protein randomly coming into existence, and that infusing it with life is many times less likely. Expanding this idea of arrangements of letters, Dr Varan gives us another perspective on the existence of DNA:

> "An enormous volume of very precise information and directions are contained in DNA. Human DNA is a sub-microscopic spiraling helix ladder with 3.2 billion pairs of nucleotide rungs (also referred to as 'letters'), with each rung carrying distinct detailed instructions... It is estimated that the DNA threads inside the body of a single person are long enough to reach the moon and back 100,000 times. The coded strings are made of common biodegradable elements. The creation of millions of miles of coded strings cannot happen by itself."

It could not just magically appear in the first place due to a flash of lightning hitting a soup of prehistoric goo. Also, it is very unlikely that the DNA code could successfully randomly mutate over time. Suppose you had a line of computer code in a working computer program. Now imagine that a one of the 1s becomes a 0. In practice the program will not be improved, and in fact it probably will no longer work at all. So the appearance of DNA in the first place is highly unlikely, and the subsequent evolution of DNA through random mutation is highly unlikely. Once again the most probable explanation is the existence of a superior intelligence "guiding" evolution, moving creation from chaos to order.

Development Timeline

This reinforces the idea of the necessity of an ordering force discussed in the previous chapter. Now let us look at some of the key events that took place regarding human development since the Big Bang. This list of key events in the development of humanity is taken from Yuval Harari's popular book *Sapiens - A Brief History of Humankind.*

1. 13.5 billion years ago: Matter and energy appear, the beginning of physics, atoms and molecules appear, the beginning of chemistry.
2. 4.5 billion years ago: Formation of planet Earth.
3. 3.8 billion years ago: Emergence of organisms. Beginning of biology.
4. 6 million years ago: Last common grandmother of humans and chimpanzees.
5. 2.5 million years ago: Evolution of the genus *Homo* in Africa. First stone tools.
6. 2 million years ago: Humans spread from Africa to Eurasia. Evolution of different human species.
7. 500,000 years ago: Neanderthals evolve in Europe and the Middle East.
8. 300,000 years ago: Daily usage of fire.
9. 200,000 years ago: *Homo sapiens* evolves in East Africa.

10. 70,000 years ago: The Cognitive Revolution. Emergence of fictive language. Beginning of history. Sapiens spread out of Africa.
11. 45,000 years ago: Sapiens settle Australia. Extinction of Australian megafauna.
12. 30,000 years ago: Extinction of Neanderthals.
13. 16,000 years ago: Sapiens settle America. Extinction of American megafauna.
14. 13,000 years ago: Extinction of *Homo floresiensis*. *Home sapiens* the only surviving human species.
15. 12,000 years ago: The Agricultural Revolution. Domestication of plants and animals. Permanent settlements.
16. 5,000 years ago: First kingdoms, script and money. Polytheistic religions.
17. 4,250 years ago: First empire - the Akkadian Empire of Sargon
18. 2,500 years ago: Invention of coinage - universal money. The Persian Empire - a universal political order 'for the benefit of all humans'. Buddhism in India - a universal truth 'to liberate all beings from suffering'.
19. 2,000 years ago: Han Empire in China. Roman Empire in the Mediterranean. Christianity.
20. 1,400 years ago: Islam.
21. 500 years ago: The Scientific Revolution. Humankind admits its ignorance and begins to acquire unprecedented power. Europeans begin to conquer America and the oceans. The entire planet becomes a single historical arena. The rise of capitalism.
22. 200 years ago: The Industrial Revolution. Family and community are replaced by state and

market. Massive extinction of plants and animals.

23. The Present: Humans transcend the boundaries of planet Earth. Nuclear weapons threaten the survival of humankind.

This is a useful timeline for understanding how far we have come since the Big Bang. These dates can be taken as the best estimates of present-day science. Some of the fossil data is very sparse, however, and may be subject to significant revision. While the book has some good factual data, it is limited by the fact that Harari explains our evolution as a series of random events. When a new level of being appears it is explained away as a genetic mutation, i.e. just another random event. But as we have already discovered the probability of such a random event is vanishingly small. Therefore the book does not help us understand the purpose our lives, which in fairness Harari never set out to do, though it is read by people who want to better understand what a human being is.

Regarding the emergence of levels of being, the mineral level appears in step 1 and life appears in step 3. The emergence of consciousness is not included in the list, probably since it is hard to put a date on this important development based on the fossil record. However we can discern the emergence of abstract thought in step 10.

Regarding step 10 - the Cognitive Revolution - Harari tells us, "Homo sapiens acquired the technology, organization skills, and perhaps even the vision necessary to break out of Afro-Asia and settle the Outer

World." Harari describes one of the events of the Cognitive Revolution as follows:

> "Their first achievement was the colonization of Australia some 45,000 years ago... The journey of the first humans to Australia is one of the most important events in history, at least as important as Columbus' journey to America or the *Apollo 11* expedition to the moon. It was the first time any human had managed to leave the Afro-Asian ecological system – indeed, the first time any large terrestrial mammal had managed to cross from Afro-Asia to Australia. Of even greater importance was what the human pioneers did in this new world. The moment the first hunter-gatherer set foot on an Australian beach was the moment that *Homo sapiens* climbed to the top rung in the food chain on a particular landmass and thereafter became the deadliest species in the annals of planet Earth."

Harari describes how apparently these early humans proceeded to wipe out large number of large mammals (steps 11 and 13). He says "Within a few thousand years, virtually all of these giants vanished. Of the twenty-four Australian animal species weighing fifty kilograms or more, twenty-three became extinct. A large number of smaller species also disappeared. Food chains throughout the entire Australian ecosystem were broken and rearranged. It was the most important transformation of the Australian ecosystem for millions of years."

It seems clear that at that point we were operating outside of the laws of nature, and therefore had emerged from the animal level of being. We had somehow acquired the capability of abstract thought and free will.

Evolution

First let us consider the process of evolution. Physical evolution is now a known fact of science. Things (including us) had different physical forms in the past. Evolution has clearly resulted in higher and higher levels of complexity on our planet, against all odds. It has already been mentioned that one of the distinguishing features of Homo sapiens (i.e. you and me) is free will, i.e. we can act outside of the rules of nature. So there we were, living our animal lives for millions of years, but then our free will appeared maybe during the Cognitive Revolution.

Developing free will and becoming "the deadliest species in the annals of planet Earth" might not be seen as something to celebrate, however we must remember that evolution is a process, meaning that we will continue to change. Let us discuss this process of evolution further to see where Homo sapiens might be heading.

There must be an ordering force behind evolution. Let us consider the example of a car factory. The products made are quite complex, and are the result of a lot of careful design work. Basic unprocessed materials go in one end of the factory and the cars come out of the other. In between is a complex process in which components and then subsystems are made and tested and then assembled into the final product. So, not only have the cars been designed, but the process for making the cars needed to be designed. Elon Musk, the head of Tesla Motors, has been known to say that the real problem is not making a car - a single prototype is easy. The real challenge is making "the machine that makes the machine", i.e. getting all of the machinery in the factory to work together to produce the desired result.

So when discussing the origins of the human race, people often feel that science has told us that we are simply the product of evolution. There is no particular reason we exist, it is just that evolution has randomly resulted in you and me. Old, dogmatic religion has tried in the past to argue that physical evolution didn't occur at all in an attempt to refute the idea that humanity evolved from apes. However in this case dogmatic elements of both science and religion are wrong. Physical evolution *has* clearly occurred, based on observed scientific data. However as discussed above, some scientists have not yet accepted the idea of a creator. The key point that remains to be understood by these scientists seems to be that the laws of probability clearly show that evolution is not random, that there must be a creator of the evolutionary process. In the above analogy, there must be a designer of the "machine that makes the machine."

Once we recognize that such a designer exists, we can look at our past with new eyes and speculate more clearly about where Homo sapiens might be headed. Hopefully "the deadliest species in the annals of planet

Earth" will not simply destroy the planet and themselves in the process.

As noted physicist Dr. Neil Turok has said "I don't think we're random - we are to some extent random of course, each of us is a random individual - but the fact that life emerged in the universe is very likely anything but a random occurrence... It sounds mystical, but I don't think that should detract from it." The fact that life, consciousness, and the capability of abstract thought are all extremely complex leads me to agree with Dr Turok when he says that "We may be the most complex things in the universe."

The Trajectory of Evolution

As we look at the evolution of the universe with the understanding a creator has been involved and has moved us along this unlikely trajectory of increasing order, what might it mean and where might it be headed?

Religion tells us that humanity is made "in the image of God": "Upon the inmost reality of each and every created thing He hath shed the light of one of His names, and made it a recipient of the glory of one of His attributes. Upon the reality of man, however, He hath focused the radiance of all of His names and attributes, and made it a mirror of His own Self. Alone of all created things man hath been singled out for so great a favor, so enduring a bounty."

The implication is that, while all of creation reflects its creator, this is particularly true of humankind. Since our creator made us (or, more precisely, designed the *process* which made us), the creator must be very complex and beyond our ability to understand (per Einstein, an "illimitable superior spirit"). If we reflect God's attributes to a greater degree than the rest of creation, then it seems likely that we are the most complex things in the universe (i.e. we are "special"). This is an important part of our understanding of our place in the universe, though admittedly it doesn't sound humble or politically correct. We will assume that this is a correct understanding, since both science and religion are pointing us in this direction.

Religion also tells us that "The learned men, that have fixed at several thousand years the life of this earth, have failed, through the long period of their observation, to consider either the number or the age of other planets... Know thou that every fixed star hath its own planets, and every planet its own creatures, whose number no man can compute." Note that this was said when the age of the earth was thought to be a few thousand years, and old religion was still clinging to that idea in spite of increasing scientific evidence to the contrary.

Regarding the Adam and Eve story, we are told "If we take this story in its apparent meaning... it is indeed extraordinary. The intelligence cannot accept it, affirm it, or imagine it; for such arrangements, such details, such speeches and reproaches are far from being those of an intelligent man, how much less of the Divinity – that Divinity who has organized this infinite universe in the most perfect form, and its innumerable inhabitants with absolute system, strength, and perfection... Therefore this story of Adam and Eve... must be thought of simply as a symbol." Indeed much of religion is symbolic and should not be interpreted literally.

Human Evolution

Since we have established the likely existence of a creator, let us try to understand our distant past while viewing it as part of a process of creation that resulted in us, along with the myriad other creatures that have come into existence. First of all it must be said that if this is true our creator must be very patient. The evolutionary process that culminated in us took a long time. If we say that we have been fully "human" since the Cognitive Revolution 70,000 years ago (step 10 in Harari's timeline above), then we have existed for only about .0005% of the time the universe has been around. Prior to that a universe came into being with orderly structure (characteristic of the mineral level), then plant life (the vegetable level), and then various creatures (i.e. the animal level).

Regarding our own development, religion tells us we can use the development of the human embryo as an analogy for the development of man as a species. From a tiny cell, the embryo passes through various stages, in some of which it really does not resemble a human being at all. At one stage the embryo even has a tail. However, at every stage it is destined to reach human form. Religion tells us:

> "...it is clear that this terrestrial globe in its present form did not come into existence all at once; but... gradually passed through different phases until it

> became adorned with its present perfection... Man, in the beginning of his existence and in the womb of the earth, like the embryo in the womb of the mother, gradually grew and developed, and passed from one form to another... It is certain that in the beginning he had not this loveliness and grace and elegance, and that he only by degrees attained this shape, this form, this beauty, and this grace... man's existence on this earth, from the beginning until it reaches this state, form, and condition, necessarily lasts a long time... But from the beginning of man's existence he is a distinct species."

The fact that we survived as a species (or a potential species) over this period of time is of course very much against the odds. The creature that eventually became us had to survive meteor strikes, ice ages, much larger and faster predators - the list goes on and on. The likelihood of the survival and development of any species is quite small. And yet we have survived and developed. This is at least some evidence that we were "meant to be." This provides encouragement and hope that our extinction as a species is not imminent!

Social Development

We could liken our development since the Cognitive Revolution to the physical development of a human embryo. Prior to the Cognitive Revolution we were embryonic, and not distinguishable from the animal level. Our goal was to survive and reproduce, without an abstract thought in our heads. An early evidence of abstract thought is the so-called Ishango bone (dated in the range of 8,000 to 20,000 years ago). This African bone has what appear to be tallying marks on it, notches carved in groups that have been explained as early lunar phase count or as an arithmetical game of some sort. Undoubtedly we were thinking abstract thoughts before then, but the Ishango bone provides clear evidence of the advent of abstract thinking.

So during our early childhood as a race we were only beginning to develop our capacity for abstract thought, but that was a real advantage over other creatures on earth - witness our domination over the creatures of Australia mentioned above (step 11 in Harari's timeline), where we misused our newly-developed powers. As our collective childhood progressed, families banded together into settlements (step 15, 12,000 years ago). We worked more cooperatively and better learned how to work with nature by learning to grow things. In late childhood villages banded together into kingdoms (step 16, 5,000 years ago). Not mentioned in Harari's timeline is the development of nations. This became common about 2,000 years ago, and in our analogy could be said to mark the beginning of humanity's period of adolescence. I would propose that we are now in the turbulent period of late adolescence.

Now as adolescents we are in the process of becoming independent adults. Nobody can tell us what to think, and we also feel we know quite a bit. However, our powers of critical reasoning are still not fully developed, and so we do not investigate things fully before forming conclusions. We are full of energy and can do a lot of damage if that energy is not rightly directed.

I had a friend who was a high school teacher, and he was very popular with his students He said that he could tell how mature his students were by looking at their eyes. Before maturity their eyes wander everywhere and are generally sort of unfocused. When his students came back to visit only a few years after graduation, their eyes would be steadier and it was clear they were much more mature. So the good news for us is that maturity seems to come relatively quickly, hopefully before we do irrecoverable damage to ourselves and the planet.

By way of encouragement, we observe that as humanity has progressed to its present state, the area of peace has steadily increased. By this I mean that in our infancy as a race, peace could be found pretty much only within our hunter-gatherer family - in our cave if you will. In our childhood, the area of peace expanded to the level of the village. Later in our collective childhood, peaceful villages combined to the level of a peaceful kingdom. Then in our early adolescence kingdoms joined and now we have (mostly) peaceful nations. The areas in which peace exists have increased. This is progress.

We can see that since the Cognitive Revolution, human life has become less brutal and longer in length. We cannot even imagine the primitive circumstances of early humans, especially since those times are not part of recorded history. But we can, for example, imagine the life of a Roman centurion (commander of 100 men). He would be told where and when to fight, and this he would do. It was unlikely that he would be alive at the end of his career to enjoy his retirement, but hey, it was a job. In this day many people can look forward to a long and peaceful life. This is progress.

We note that it has not been an easy or fast process. If you had talked to a villager in Gaul in the Middle Ages and told him or her that they would eventually be joining together with other kingdoms to form the great and peaceful nation of France, he or she would have laughed and called the idea utterly impractical, mostly because it was difficult to imagine the steps required for it to happen.

It seems clear that the next step for the human race is to have peace on a global level, where nations will join together and form an international governing body sufficient to address and regulate global concerns (e.g. climate change, international banking and trade, caring for the seas, etc.). This won't be easy and the precise way forward is not clear, but global organization is not optional (see below). Hopefully in a few more centuries we will become "mature", which is not a long time compared to the last 70,000 years.

Let us use the analogy of an electrical power station. It is a complex process, with many subsystems (fuel supply, water supply, turbine control, generator control, etc.) that can and do function correctly. But there must be a small system sitting at the top that sends commands to co-ordinate the functions of the subsystems. Without this small system the power station will not work - it will not produce any electricity at all. We can compare the various subsystems to the nations of the world, and the earth to the entire power station. The condition of the world today shows us that without some kind of organization at the global level, global issues cannot be resolved, to the detriment of the nations. It is becoming clear that "the earth is but one country, and mankind its citizens", and we need an organization to deal with world-level issues. This is not optional and will eventually come to pass, though it is hard to imagine the steps it will take.

Spiritual Development

There also is another interesting trend that we propose can be seen since the Cognitive Revolution. When we were in the animal condition, before we evolved to have free will and abstract thought, we were "hardwired" to the laws of Nature. This meant we were acting according to the laws of our creator, and this was not optional (no free will, remember?). But then sometime around the Cognitive Revolution our latent free will became operative, and all bets were off. We could do whatever we wanted, and we had to *figure out* how to run our lives. Religion gave us moral guidance (per Harari's step 18) which we learned to apply, and so we used our free will to learn and carry out the guidance of our creator to a degree, along with any other ideas we had (which unfortunately included wars and conquest).

I have already indicated that there were periods of a few centuries after each great religion was founded where civilization flourished, and I proposed that this was because we were still positively influenced by the moral force inherent in religion. Societies would advance, but then this positive influence would fade as man-made ideas crept into religion. Social conditions also changed over the centuries, and these two factors created a situation where new moral guidance would be needed, and a new religion would come and the process would repeat.

Religion has evolved along with humanity. In earlier times religions teachings were relatively simple, and suited to basic, illiterate societies. For example the Ten Commandments provided simple, understandable moral guidance. Now we have more advanced religious teachings such as gender and race equality, the oneness of religion, and the oneness of humanity.

One theory to consider is this: we have now matured sufficiently such that each individual can become responsible for his or her spiritual development. This means that eventually we will probably no longer need a priesthood, which of course was needed back when a vast majority of people were illiterate. It also means that we all have the responsibility to independently investigate spiritual truth on our own. The good news is that truth is out there waiting to be discovered, and when we discover any truth on our own it means a lot more to us, and it is highly motivating. So the trend I propose is this: we have been on a long journey back to God since we left the natural world tens of thousands of years ago. We lived according to the laws of creation back then, and we are heading toward a situation where individuals will use their free will to discover and live by the laws of creation once again (where God's will "will be done on earth as it is in heaven").

This points to a very positive future for the human race. We will be living in peace on a global level, and we will not be abusing the planet. There will be racial and gender harmony. This is fundamentally because we will have a better material/spiritual balance in society. This idea is supported by the following statement from religion:

> "At the heart of the divisions in society today is a crisis of identity. The way people think about who they are and how they see their place in the world determine how they relate to others and what they regard as their individual and collective purpose. [It is God] who defines human nature and purpose, [who] describes the purpose of life as essentially spiritual in nature... The soul has no gender, no ethnicity, no race. God sees no differences among human beings except in relation to the conscious effort of each individual to purify his or her soul and to express its full powers. In God's sight, all human beings are as one and have the common duty of knowing and worshiping Him and contributing to advancing civilization. This truth is directly related to another - that humanity is one family."

It is proposed that this is where we are heading spiritually. This brings us to our discussion of purpose in life.

Aa Bb Cc Dd Ee Ff Gg
RULE #1
OBEY
MISS O'BRIEN

Chapter 4 – Meaning and Purpose

This is not a huge chapter, mostly because in broad terms our purpose in life is not a complicated thing.

Background

My wife used to teach childbirth classes, and afterwards would sometimes invite the new mothers to attend what she called "spiritual mothering classes." One of the mothers made the frank admission that she would have a hard time teaching her child what was right and wrong, since she herself wasn't so sure. Wouldn't it be nice to be able to confidently respond to our children concerning the big questions of life? This book proposes a framework for understanding life which, if true, will certainly be beneficial to us and our children.

We have established that in all likelihood there is a creator, as well as some kind of life after this one. It is also reasonable to believe that a creator knows the purpose of the created thing. Now the question arises as to whether *our* creator has anything to say about the purpose of our existence. This information would logically come from religion, but unfortunately "old" religion (with its dogmatic and inflexible interpretations of what God has said) has discredited itself, and relatively "new" science (with its rapidly evolving understandings and rather adolescent confidence) has told us to disregard religion. Let us re-examine whether or not religion has something useful to offer.

I propose that human purpose needs to be a) common to all, and b) comprehensible by all.

If it is not common to all, then chaos is the natural result. In today's society we tend to do our own thing, and this is fundamentally good. Independent thought is one of the hallmarks of science, helping it to advance rapidly. However, it is clear that *common* understandings are necessary for society to function peacefully and effectively, which necessarily means that "our own thing" needs to be done within a framework. This is true in science, where the peer-review process provides a forum for all to come to common scientific understandings. Let us consider a sports team. All the players and coaches understand the objectives (purpose) of the sport. If they did not, there would be chaos on the pitch. Even if only one player didn't understand the game, things would not go well.

As we mature and come to the conclusion that humanity is an organic whole, then we will realize that if there is a person or a society that is not healthy, then the world itself is not healthy, which means that even though we might live somewhere else, we are actually part of a "sick" society. Therefore it makes sense to work to bring health to that person or society. Consider the human body - suppose you have an infected finger. It is then a simple fact that you are not healthy, even though only a fraction of your entire body is not well. Health is not possible unless other parts of your body come to the rescue. Your entire body has a common purpose and works to deal with the infection. What would happen if the white blood cells decided they would "look out for number one" and focus only on their own needs? The natural result would be the death of the entire body, including the white blood cells.

Common purpose is necessary and logical for the good of all.

Since we are all unique individuals, the way that we carry out our purpose will vary, but we need that common framework to define our lives. A word of caution: finding out what to do with your life is not the same as finding out what your life is about. The former is very personal, but the latter needs to be agreed by all of us.

The second requirement for human purpose is that it must be comprehensible. A common purpose is no good if a portion of humanity doesn't know what it means in practical terms. It must be something that *all* of us can apply in our everyday lives. Therefore it cannot be something that is intellectually complicated or too abstract. We shouldn't need a university education to understand the purpose of our lives.

So now, finally, to the heart of the matter. We have already established that there is a creator and that the creator of anything knows its purpose. So what does our creator say about our purpose?

Our Two Duties

When I was a small child, I would sometimes watch my father shave, standing on a small stool. One day I found myself in his bathroom by myself. I took out the stool and used it to look at myself in the mirror, and had what was possibly my first philosophical thought. I pulled on my face, thinking "That's me, but that's not ME. What is ME is what is looking out of these eyes." In my own childish way, I had realized that my spirit or soul was distinct from my body. Since we have a spirit, then of course our purpose must relate to that as well.

Not only should we find purpose in life, our creator says it is our duty to do so.

> "The first duty prescribed by God for His servants is the recognition of Him Who is the Dayspring of His Revelation and the Fountain of His laws, Who representeth the Godhead in both the Kingdom of His Cause and the world of creation. Whoso achieveth this duty hath attained unto all good."

This seems to say that we first need to find the source of guidance for our lives. We all live together in this world, with all of the challenges that entails. It sometimes feels as if we are in a dark tunnel, stumbling about, trying to make our way out of the tunnel. The person who sees the light at the end of the tunnel has an advantage and can make progress, while the rest cannot. We propose that God's messengers (the founders of the world's great religions) have been the source of that light. Once we recognize this light source, we can move on to our second duty (there are only two), which is to make our way toward that light.

> "...It behooveth everyone who reacheth this most sublime station, this summit of transcendent glory, (i.e. recognizing Moses, Krishna, Buddha, Christ, Muhammad, Bahá'u'lláh, etc.) to observe every ordinance of Him Who is the Desire of the world. These twin duties are inseparable."

So once we recognize our source of guidance, we try to do all that that being says. This of course is a never-ending task, since it is impossible to be e.g. perfectly honest or perfectly forgiving. It is no help to accept one duty and not the other, since we don't get the guidance without the first duty, and the guidance has no result unless we attempt the second.

It was mentioned above that all creatures except humanity naturally operate according to the will of God. In these two duties we are asked to use our free will to a) recognize the source of God's will and b) carry out God's will as best we can. In that way the human race will approach a seminal moment in the history of the planet, when *all* created beings will at least try to operate according to the will of God. This will mark the maturation of the human race. At present we are in our tumultuous adolescence, so it is hard to imagine that we can achieve this. Yet history suggests that religion has an in-built power to transform individuals and society, especially in the early days of a given religion. We can have hope that in this day such a power will help us to achieve, for the first and only time, a purposeful sustainable world civilization.

Knowing God

Also, regarding purpose, religion tells us: "I bear witness, O my God, that Thou hast created me to know Thee and to worship Thee." This is similar to the two duties mentioned above.

It is proposed that our primary means of knowing God is to know his manifestation or messenger (other things which facilitate knowing God are discussed below and in Appendix 2). The second thing we are told to do in the above passage is to worship God. Religion tells us "This is worship: to serve mankind and to minister to the needs of the people." So in the previous short passage we see that our purpose is both spiritual and practical. We will consider this further below.

Following God's guidance is not a mindless thing. It is similar to when we are trying to drive from one place to another using a GPS. It has reliably gotten us to many other locations, so we accept it as our source of guidance. We have faith in our GPS and do what it tells us, but it is not blind faith, it is faith based on experience. As we discover the positive benefits of following God's guidance, our understanding and faith in it will grow. Future generations will probably regard this perspective as obvious. At present we are not engaging with God's guidance, and so faith is often not an experienced thing for many people. We leave matters of faith to a priesthood (who we usually ignore...).

One way we can know God is by observing his creation. In the same way we begin to be able to recognize and admire the traits of a master artist through his or her works, i.e. we see the artist in the work of art, we are able to know God by observing his creation.

It is said that "Every created thing in the whole universe is but a door leading into His knowledge", thus we shall say that creation is designed to help humanity know and love God. Here are other statements that support this concept:

- "...not a single atom in the entire universe can be found which doth not declare the evidences of His might"
- "Whatever is in the heavens and whatever is on the earth is a direct evidence of the revelation within it of the attributes and names of God, inasmuch as within every atom are enshrined the signs that bear eloquent testimony to the revelation of that Most Great Light...... How resplendent the luminaries of knowledge that shine in an atom, and how vast the oceans of wisdom that surge within a drop!... From that which hath been said it becometh evident that all things, in their inmost reality, testify to the revelation of the names and attributes of God within them. Each according to its capacity, indicateth, and is expressive of, the knowledge of God."
- "Know thou that every created thing is a sign of the revelation of God. Each, according to its capacity, is, and will ever remain, a token of the Almighty. Inasmuch as He, the sovereign Lord of all, hath willed to reveal His sovereignty in the kingdom of names and attributes, each and every created thing hath, through the act of the Divine Will, been made a sign of His glory. So pervasive and general is this revelation that nothing whatsoever in the whole universe can be discovered that doth not reflect His splendor."

God's messengers represent God to us, so knowing them is effectively knowing God. They are like perfect mirrors, reflecting the light and heat of the sun (God).

So another way we can know God is by studying the lives of God's messengers. Our love for these messengers increases as we come to understand how they have suffered for our sake. Better understanding of the sacrifice they made out of love for us deepens our knowledge and love of God. We must be careful to not be like the farmer in Chapter 2, rejecting a visitor without sufficient investigation.

Another way we can get to know someone is by talking with them, and prayer is conversation with God. It is more difficult to love someone that you seldom communicate with. So praying helps us know God. Prayer is a natural urge. For example when we are suddenly surprised or in danger, we often immediately say "Oh my God!". This is a supplication, a prayer. A heart connecting to its creator is not an intellectual thing.

Another way to get to know God's messengers is to read what they wrote and meditate upon it. When we meditate on these writings new horizons of knowledge are opened to us. When we develop our own insights in this way our faith (confidence in the GPS) is strengthened. This process of personal transformation that naturally occurs through prayer and meditation means that we become more God-like (i.e. we become better people), and in this way we can also better appreciate and know God.

Acquiring virtues and serving humanity

A wise man was asked "What is the purpose of our lives?" He replied "To acquire virtues." This supports the original proposal regarding our purpose in this life, i.e.

Our common purpose: to develop ourselves spiritually in preparation for the next life

This purpose is common to every human being. As we transform spiritually - developing spiritual attributes such as compassion, justice, patience, and perseverance - we become better people. We become more pleasant to be with.

We have already discussed the existence of a next life. It is clear that the only thing we take with us is our soul or spirit (the thing that makes us us). This being the case, then we want our soul to be as well-developed as possible to better enjoy the next life.

As mentioned before, this world is like a womb, where we develop spiritually in the same way that a child develops physically in the womb of the mother before it is born. An important distinction is that in the womb of the mother, our free will is not used to help us develop - this happens according to natural law. However in this life, our spirit will develop in proportion to the efforts we make to develop it. This life is a workshop, not an art gallery! In addition to this, the events of our lives, both good and bad, help to develop us spiritually. This world is the perfect spiritual womb. We don't want to be born into the next life handicapped. If the child in the womb does not fully develop physically, through no fault of its own it is born handicapped. Its physical condition often cannot be improved after it is born. The same is true of our condition when we arrive in the next life. If we have neglected our spiritual development in this life, it is likely we cannot improve it in the next life. A scary but motivating thought.

One of the interesting things about spiritual development we find is that "the more we know, the more we know we don't know", and so we also become more humble. This is consistent with the experience of the scientist - consider the Einstein quote earlier in the book. Humility is not a common attribute of adolescence, but will become very common in a mature society.

We have already discussed levels of being, and how the Manifestations of God (the founders of the world's great religions) are above us and therefore we can never fully know them. We are told that the highest achievement for a human being is attaining the station of servitude - serving God by serving our fellow human beings. In effect we can become channels through which God's love reaches others. By achieving our natural place in the order of things (as servants of society), we become happier. A few quotations from various religions about becoming a servant of society can be found in Appendix 1, and they sound remarkably similar. On the basis of these quotations we can understand the second aspect of our purpose:

Your particular purpose: to develop your talents and capacities for use in service to humanity

We are all born with talents and capacities. It aids our spiritual development to use these to be of service to your fellow man. For example, we should try to develop the spiritual attribute of generosity. We can only do this by being with and being generous to others - we cannot do it alone.

By becoming service-minded we develop ourselves spiritually and at the same time we help carry forward an ever-advancing civilization. We need to work to optimize the conditions of society for spiritual development, and advance civilization sustainably such that future generations can also effectively make their pilgrimage through this life. Helping to reduce poverty, improve agriculture, reduce disease, reduce the impact of natural disasters, helping others achieve their potential, etc. are effective ways to serve civilization. Basically we should, through volunteer work, our professions, and in our daily lives, be focused on the good of others while also providing for the needs of our families. The specifics are left to the individual, based on their talents and opportunities.

If we become service-minded, then throughout the day even the smallest act of kindness shown to someone becomes an act of service. My wife is always looking to help others - to cheer their hearts. She might just call or visit someone who is having difficulties, and she knows this is a service that is in harmony with her life purpose. She is also a poet, and when she reads her poetry it is not to feed her ego – she knows it might uplift someone's spirit, which of course is a service. We always taught our children to be "helpers", and observed how happy they became when helping others. When I was a young engineer, an older colleague, as an act of kindness, advised me that during the course of my career that I should always "look out for number one". I thanked him for his kindness, while knowing this commonly-believed concept was false. It was not in line with my life purpose.

It is interesting to note that pretty much any unselfish act can be a service. For example you may not enjoy your present occupation, but you grind your way through the day because supporting your family is an important service. Even the same job can be a service when performed by one person and a selfish act when performed by another. For example, suppose you are a financial advisor. If you advise your client with the primary goal of maximizing your commission, then you are not being of service. In the same job you might focus on your client's well-being and the natural result is benefit to you. Whether or not something is a service can be down to your frame of mind.

You are probably performing many services already, either at work or at home, though you might not put it in the context of your life purpose. In any case I congratulate you, because you are acting in accordance with the will of your creator and helping to achieve part of your purpose on this earth.

So it might be said that we have a twofold moral purpose: 1) to take charge of our own spiritual development and 2) to serve others and contribute to the transformation of society. These two purposes are complementary. By doing the first we can better do the second, and by doing the second we help achieve the first. One is inward-looking and the other is outward-looking, which seems a nice balance. We can also think of this as the balance between *being* (acquiring virtues) and *doing* (performing acts of service).

Our Twofold Moral Purpose

We restate our purpose as follows: 1) to take charge of our own spiritual growth, and 2) to contribute to the transformation of society through selfless service.

It seems a good time to say that this book is one of the ways in which I am trying to serve society. As has been said, society is in the process of leaving adolescence. I believe people will be giving more and more mature thought to life purpose, and this book is a contribution to that process. I remember one time having a discussion with the head of the college where I lectured, and suggesting to him that we should offer a module on the subject of life purpose. I thought it could and maybe should be part of a well-rounded education, and would open up some interesting discussions. However he felt that such a subject was not suitable to people of that age. Maybe he was right in the sense that adolescents are often too busy expending their abundant energy to think much about such things. However the logic of such an exploration cannot be denied, and we should probably think about life purpose at all stages of our lives.

If we actually believe that we are going to be born into another life for which our soul needs to be developed, it makes sense to make the development of our soul a key priority in this life. For most people this means a bit of a re-orientation of their lives. What might this look like?

If we go back to the thoughts of my boss at the beginning of the book, he viewed his life as a game that he wanted to play and win. Winning seemed to involve accumulating more and more material wealth. Any development of his soul along the way would happen by chance, not by any particular efforts on his part. It is actually dangerous to focus on material well-being alone, because you may unintentionally hinder the development of your soul. For example, one of the qualities we should be developing is generosity, but a materialistic lifestyle actively fosters greed, which stunts the development of the soul.

When I left that job, it wasn't because I disliked my boss. I just wanted to live a meaningful life, being of use to the world, so I embarked into the world of renewable energy engineering, where I unknowingly was actively fulfilling part two of my twofold moral purpose. The funny thing is that I could have stuck with that original job, and with a simple change of perspective would have been pursuing my twofold moral purpose without a career change, since that job could also have been viewed as a service. It just seemed meaningless at the time.

Let us talk a bit more about this second part of our twofold moral purpose (contributing to and serving society). Living our lives in an attitude of service to others is something that everyone can do, regardless of education, intellect, or life circumstances. I could have been of more assistance to my workmates, been more helpful around the house, joined the Tidy Towns Committee etc without changing jobs! Such a lifestyle requires self-sacrifice, but when we understand that it is our purpose to be of service we simply get on with it, and soon find that we are happy. For a human being, deep happiness seems a by-product of service, a by-product of being what we are meant to be. It cannot be pursued directly (e.g. take a happiness course). When a robin joins the dawn chorus on a spring morning, I would like to think that its song of joy simply comes as a by-product of living in harmony with the will of its creator. See Appendix 2 for thoughts on the idea if that all of creation (including us) operated according to God's will, we would have a sustainable society.

Earlier we talked about levels of being, and one of the key characteristics of the human level of being is service. Once again you are referred to Appendix 1. We note that while we can and generally do come up with our own ideas for being of service, we should probably also seek out the ways in which our creator wants us to be of service. Such ideas can be found in the teachings of each religion, and I leave the investigation to you. As an example, in the Bahá'í faith people work to provide spiritual education programs to all, to help redress the present material/spiritual imbalance in society.

Having briefly discussed the second part of our twofold moral purpose, how do we accomplish the first part (advancing ourselves spiritually)? Following God's guidance is not a mindless thing. We often think that we know what God wants of us, without actually reading what He has to say. This once again is a characteristic of adolescence. We obviously need to *find out* what God has to say to us about how we might advance spiritually. We don't somehow magically just know. How do we do this?

A Covenant

Whether we know it or not, we have an agreement - a covenant - with our creator, and it goes something like this. God says "Try to do what I say, and all will be well." This is not unlike when we first go to school (refer to the illustration at the beginning of the chapter). A lovely analogy is given as follows:

> "The relationship of God with man in this Covenant is somewhat similar to the relationship between the principal of a school and the child. As soon as a child goes to school for the first time, he enters into a covenant with the school principal, although often without really knowing it. In this contract the principal provides the means for the education of the child. He appoints teachers to teach him, draws up the educational programme and ensures the child's well-being and development in every way. The child's part in this covenant is to follow the instructions of the teacher and learn every lesson he is taught. It is through this process that the child acquires

intellectual and spiritual powers. As the child grows in learning and maturity, the principal will appoint other teachers to contribute to his education. In this covenant, the responsibilities of the two parties are fundamentally different. They cannot be confused and are not interchangeable.

"Another feature of this covenant is that the two parties are not of the same caliber. One side, the school principal, is knowledgeable, wise and strong. The other, the child, is unlearned, weak and immature. The terms of this covenant are drawn up entirely by the strong party and the child has no say in them. Usually, the weaker party is the loser when a contract is drawn up solely by the strong. Not so in this case, for the motive of the principal in making all the arrangements is his love for the child and concern for its education. His greatest ambition is to see the child attain wisdom and knowledge...

"The same is true of God. He is the Creator, and Almighty, the Author of the Covenant, whose terms He Himself has stipulated unilaterally without the help of man. As in the above example, God's part in this Covenant is different from man's."

In the above analogy, God's messengers (Buddha, Krishna, Moses, Christ, Bahá'u'lláh, etc., i.e. the founders of the world's great religions) are our teachers, and God is the principal. They bring the guidance of our creator to us, so knowing them is effectively knowing God. They are like perfect mirrors, reflecting God to us.

As discussed, it is proposed that in this life we have only two duties: 1) to recognize God's messengers (i.e. find the source of information that guides our lives) and 2) then do what they say. This of course means making the effort to *find out* what they say.

God's part of this covenant is to arrange the affairs of our lives in such a way that we have opportunities for spiritual development, in preparation for the next life. We should be thankful for this and be aware of what is happening, knowing that whatever happens can in the long run only be good for us (at least in a spiritual sense). My in-laws always said "things work out for the best", and there is a profound wisdom in this statement.

Final Thoughts on Purpose

So there it is. If you think these ideas are reasonable, your immediate action (if you are not already doing so) is to read the writings of the great religions and meditate on them with your heart and mind. Then figure out how to implement these teachings in your daily life.

You are in effect building a framework within which to conduct your life. Like any framework it will have a stabilizing effect on your life, enabling you to better understand and deal with its inevitable challenges. In these ways you will be better developed for when you arrive in the next life. Enjoy!

OIL

Chapter 5 - Our Role in the Natural World

Let's take a break from the idea of purpose, returning to it in the final chapter. In this chapter we investigate the positive implications for the natural world that will naturally (!) follow in a society that has found a material/spiritual balance. This is further considered in Appendix 2.

How will we think of nature in the future, in a world that understands its purpose, and what are the potential benefits to the planet? As already mentioned above, we will have a spiritual perspective, as embodied in the following: "Every created thing in the whole universe is but a door leading into his (God's) knowledge."

We are presently mistreating nature in various ways (pollution, rain forest destruction, etc.). We live in a world that is unbalanced in that there is a big emphasis on material development, and insufficient emphasis on spiritual development, i.e. we are materialistic. This has, among other things, brought about a crisis in the natural world, which we are unsuccessfully dealing with. Why and how are we spoiling the very womb from which we are born into the next life?

The primary reasons for this seem to be that we are morally rudderless as well as ignorant of our purpose. The idea of right and wrong isn't sufficiently clear when compared to the demands of economics, where the bottom line or responsibility to shareholders is the dominant focus. In the business world, if you are operating ethically and your competitors are not, then you may end up going out of business. At present the tendency is to talk about sustainability, but do very little about it. On a positive note, the fact that we have at least begun to talk about sustainability is a welcome development, and a sign that we are maturing.

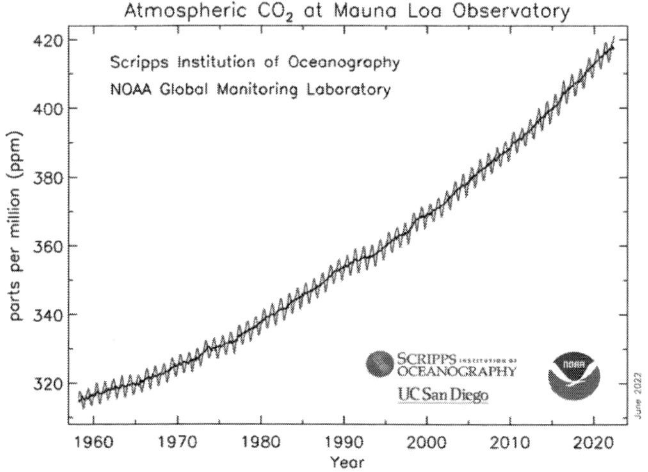

For example, we have known about global warming since the 1980s. Noted astronomer and visionary Carl Sagan testified before the US Congress in 1985 on the subject. The graph above shows our rate of progress in reducing CO_2 emissions (i.e. no progress, the graph should be relatively flat at some low level, but it is going up at an ever-increasing rate). But you can't fool Mother Nature. This will bring about inevitable consequences.

There is no real business incentive to reduce emissions, except for a few limited government sanctions. In the long run, this is suicidal behavior, i.e. it is illogical. We would behave more logically a) if we were more ethical, b) if we knew why we are here in the first place, and c) if we had a functional global framework for dealing with global problems.

There are numerous similar global environmental crises that could be mentioned, which are not being addressed largely because it doesn't make short term economic sense to do so. These crises are the natural result of a society that is immersed in materialism, i.e. a society that is lacking a spiritual/material balance. We are treating nature as an economic asset. This fits into our purely materialistic understanding of this life. In our ignorant, enthusiastic adolescence we are running like lemmings for the cliff.

Nature

A dictionary definition of nature is "The forces or processes of the physical world, generally personified as a female being" (e.g. Mother Earth, Mother Nature). It can also be defined as "the material world."

As discussed previously, the physical world is an incubator or womb. It is a place where we exercise our free will to develop qualities and attributes which will be of use to us both here and in the next life. So we are born from this life - from the Earth, from the natural world - into the next. Therefore we see how appropriate it is to personify nature as being female.

Although nature reflects the attributes of God, nature is not part of God. We are reminded of the story of the dervish who was cooking his meal and incorrectly explained that he was "cooking God." The response of a passing wise man was "Such an error hath been committed by certain foolish ones who [have concluded] that all created things are the signs of God, and that, consequently, there is no distinction whatsoever between them... [but] Everything besides Him is as nothing..." And again religion says "Regard thou the one true God as One Who is apart from, and immeasurably exalted above, all created things. The whole universe reflecteth His glory, while He is Himself independent of, and transcendeth His creatures."

As we observe nature we begin to understand the idea of the unity of creation, because it becomes apparent that all of nature is interconnected. Try to imagine a room full of balls connected and suspended by springs. If we tap any one ball, the effect will eventually affect all the others. Similarly tossing a pebble into a still pond eventually affects the whole pond. "...Every created thing hath, according to a fixed decree, been endowed with the capacity to exercise a particular influence, and been made to possess a distinct virtue."

Our relationship with nature is an interesting one. Physically we are part of nature - we must eat, we must sleep and deal with the many other demands associated with our physical selves. Indeed we can observe in our physical selves the evidences of a creator in the same way we observe them in the rest of the natural world. "How resplendent the luminaries of knowledge that shine in an atom, and how vast the oceans of wisdom that surge within a drop! To a supreme degree is this true of man, who, among all created things, hath been invested with the robe of such gifts, and hath been singled out for the glory of such distinction. For in him are potentially revealed all the attributes and names of God to a degree that no other created being hath excelled or surpassed. All these names and attributes are applicable to him..."

We are told that creation is perfect. "So perfect and comprehensive is His creation that no mind nor heart, however keen or pure, can ever grasp the nature of the most insignificant of His creatures." And yet we read elsewhere that nature is <u>im</u>perfect! "Nature is the material world. When we look upon it, we see that it is dark and imperfect. For instance, if we allow a piece of land to remain in its natural condition, we will find it covered with thorns and thistles; useless weeds and wild vegetation will flourish upon it, and it will become like a jungle. The trees will be fruitless, lacking beauty and symmetry; wild animals, noxious insects and reptiles will abound in its dark recesses. This is the incompleteness and imperfection of the world of nature."

These two statements can be resolved when we realize that there is more to creation than nature. What completes the picture? What "added ingredient" results in the perfection of creation? When we discussed levels of being we noted that human beings can (for better or for worse) operate outside of the laws of nature. So it is proposed that nature plus humanity has the potential to result in a perfect creation.

It is said that "...it (nature) is, nevertheless, imperfect because it has need of intelligence and education... Education is a necessity. If a piece of ground be left in its natural and original state, it will either become a thorny waste or be covered by worthless weeds. When cleared and cultivated, this same unproductive field will yield plentiful harvests of food." This implies that it is man's lot to "interfere" with nature.

"God has deposited within the human creature an illimitable power by which he can rule the world of nature." For example, on our own we are incapable of flight, but by better understanding the physical and natural world we can fly via aircraft. A human being "...discovers latent realities within the bosom of the earth, uncovers treasures, penetrates secrets and mysteries of the phenomenal world and brings to light that which according to nature's jealous laws should remain hidden, unknown and unfathomable. Through an ideal inner power man brings these realities forth from the invisible plane to the visible. This is contrary to nature's law."

The beauty of formal gardens is "symbolic of the nature of the transformation which is destined to occur both within the hearts of the world's peoples and in the physical environment of the planet." From them we get a glimpse of how working with nature will help make this world a material and spiritual paradise. Religion predicts such changes will likely occur, for example in the Lord's prayer, which expresses the hope that society will operate according to the will of God. Of course it will take centuries to achieve, but a few centuries are as nothing compared to how long we've been around.

Attitudes Toward Nature

Therefore we are intended to influence the natural world and not simply to fit into the forces of nature, as important as that is. This is a key point, and one that many environmentally conscious people might find hard to accept. With this fact of dominance goes a responsibility to act with wisdom, something we are failing to do at the moment. We are presently dominating as ruthless and ignorant dictators, whereas we should be loving and reverent caretakers. We should "Look not upon the creatures of God (i.e. all that is created) except with the eye of kindliness and of mercy, for Our loving providence hath pervaded all created things, and Our grace encompassed the earth and the heavens."

First of all this material world is a creation of our creator, deserving of reverent care and conservation. When we think of those first photographs of the earth taken from outer space, we realize it is a precious blue and white gem, more awe-inspiring than the most beautiful work of art, and it should be treated as such. Secondly it is our common womb. The conditions of the womb certainly affect the child within it, and so we must help optimize the conditions of this world for our spiritual growth.

It is daunting to think of the wisdom this will require. At the present time we are comparatively ignorant of the complex interrelationships of the natural world, and because of this we should become more careful when we exercise influence over nature. But because managing the natural environment will require detailed knowledge of creation and therefore the Creator, this responsibility will help us fulfill our life purpose.

The State of the World

The present condition of the physical world seems to be a reflection of the spiritual condition of humanity - it is in crisis. Forests are shrinking, deserts are growing and soil is eroding – all at record rates. Thousands of species disappear annually. Pollution of many kinds is growing worse. It is clearly understood that global warming is occurring, is man-made, and is a threat to human civilization.

The environmental crisis is one of many interrelated crises facing the world today – and an integrated solution is required. The UN World Commission on Environment and Development was so-named because it is impossible to separate social development issues and environmental issues. Their 1985 landmark report *Our Common Future* states: "The next few decades are crucial. The time has come to break out of past patterns. Attempts to maintain social and ecological stability through old approaches to development and environmental protection will increase instability.

Security must be sought through change. The Commission has noted a number of actions that must be taken to reduce risks to survival and to put future development on paths that are sustainable. Yet we are aware that such a reorientation on a continuing basis is simply beyond the reach of present decision-making structures and institutional arrangements, both national and international."

Religion tells us "If long-cherished ideals and time-honored institutions, if certain social assumptions and religious formulae have ceased to promote the welfare of the generality of mankind, if they no longer minister to the needs of a continually evolving humanity, let them be swept away and relegated to the limbo of obsolescent and forgotten doctrines. Why should these, in a world subject to the immutable law of change and decay, be exempt from the deterioration that must needs overtake every human institution? For legal standards, political and economic theories are solely designed to safeguard the interests of humanity as a whole, and not humanity to be crucified for the preservation of the integrity of any particular law or doctrine." The deterioration of the environment is heightening public awareness of the inability of present social and political systems to cope with a changing world, and forcing movement toward a more formalized world civilization.

The following statements from *Our Common Future* put the situation in perspective. "...These developing countries must operate in a world in which the resources gap between most developing and industrial nations is widening, in which the industrial world dominates in the rule-making of some key international bodies, and in which the industrial world has already used much of the planet's ecological capital. This inequality is the planet's main 'environmental' problem... Most of these countries face enormous economic pressures, both international and domestic, to overexploit their environmental resource base." This is obviously unjust and is a moral/spiritual problem.

Religion tells us "Whoso cleaveth to justice, can, under no circumstances, transgress the limits of moderation. He discerneth the truth in all things, through the guidance of Him Who is the All-Seeing. The civilization, so often vaunted by the learned exponents of arts and sciences, will, if allowed to overleap the bounds of moderation, bring great evil upon men... If carried to excess, civilization will prove as prolific a source of evil as it had been of goodness when kept within the restraints of moderation."

Present day society is immoderate, and is unsustainable environmentally, socially, politically, and spiritually. National politics are inadequate for a world civilization. Neither capitalism nor socialism have proven adequate to deal with the demands of society today. "The time has come when those who preach the dogmas of materialism, whether of the east or the west, whether of capitalism or socialism, must give account of the moral stewardship they have presumed to exercise. Where is the 'new world' promised by these ideologies? Where is the international peace to whose ideals they proclaim their devotion? Where are the breakthroughs into new realms of cultural achievement produced by the aggrandizement of this race, of that nation or of a particular class? Why is the vast majority of the world's peoples sinking ever deeper into hunger and wretchedness when wealth on a scale undreamed of by the Pharaohs, the Caesars, or even the imperialist powers of the nineteenth century is at the disposal of the present arbiters of human affairs?"

Global institutions

It is clear that the integrated and interdependent nature of the new challenges and issues contrasts sharply with the nature of the institutions that exist today. We have technological tools to deal with a world society but at present lack institutions which they can serve.

There is plenty of evidence that we are physically able to sustain a world civilization. Infant mortality is falling, life expectancy is increasing, the proportion of the world's adults who can read and write is climbing, and the proportion of children starting school is rising. It seems to be a question of needing a better spiritual/material balance, and a world organization that is capable of managing global needs (leaving national and local needs to national and local governments).

Undoubtedly we can find ways to help society carry forward an ever-advancing civilization, some of which have to do with environmental conservation. We can also modify our individual lifestyles to have less impact on the environment. This becomes much easier when we see the big picture - what our own lives are about and the purpose of the natural world around us. In particular if we understand that we are only passing through on our way to the next life, it becomes easier to take a long-term view of actions needed to leave the planet in a suitable condition for generations yet unborn. Our individual demand for more and more material goods will level out.

Even if the path to our goal is not clear to us (just like the Gauls in Chapter 3!), we will increasingly work together to improve society, and this time with knowledge of a common purpose. We will develop for the first and only time in human history a peaceful, sustainable global civilization.

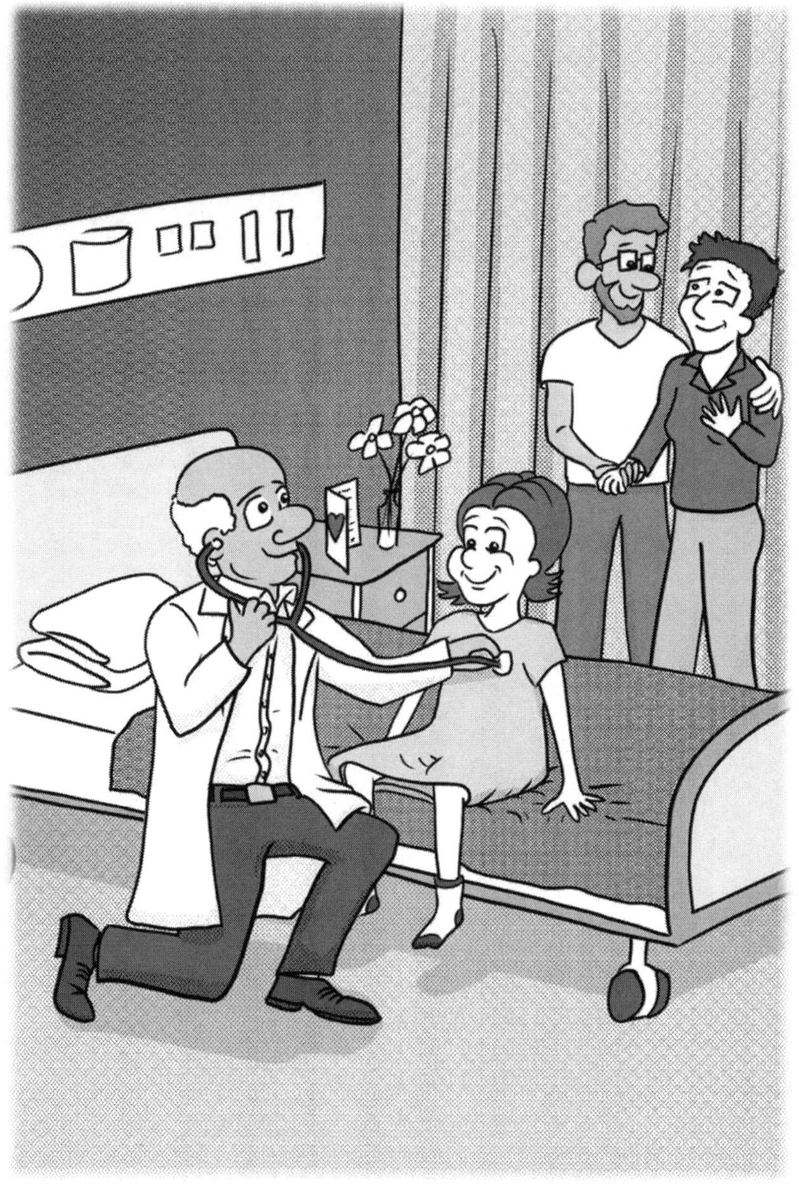

Chapter 6 - Conclusion

Anything we do, we do for a reason. It is unreasonable to do anything without knowing what it is you are trying to accomplish. Hence knowledge of the purpose of your life seems fundamental to your existence on this earth. However it is a subject that most people haven't yet considered deeply, partially because it is assumed there is no real answer. This book attempts to put together a coherent discussion of the subject, though of course not everyone would approach it this way. Hopefully at least some of it has been useful to the reader!

Let us summarize the key points that have been developed:

- Whenever we try to increase our knowledge on any subject, we are rewarded with insights. This includes seeking knowledge of purpose.
- Order in the universe is extremely improbable, and the existence of order implies the existence of an ordering force.
- Our universe has a creator, i.e. a creation presupposes a creator
- There are different "levels of being" in this life (mineral, vegetable, animal, human), and there are probably levels above us which we are incapable of fully understanding.
- We are probably the most complex things in the universe
- We have a limited understanding of the properties which separate the different levels of being, i.e. life, consciousness, and the capacity

for abstract thinking, and cannot replicate them. In general, we actually know very little of what there is to be known. "The more you know, the more you know you don't know."

- Pure religious teachings are guidance from our creator, and should be central to our search for meaning in life ("when all else fails, read the instructions").
- It is likely that we go on in some fashion after we die, to a condition we can only dimly visualize in this life.
- The human race has matured sufficiently such that each individual can now become responsible for his or her spiritual development.
- Human purpose needs to be a) common to all, and b) comprehensible by all.
- ***The purpose that is common to all of us is that we should develop ourselves spiritually in preparation for the next life (i.e. we should take charge of our own spiritual growth).***
- ***The purpose that is different for each person is the development your unique talents and capacities to serve society.***

The human race has been around for a long time. At some stage we emerged from the animal level, when we developed free will. Prior to this we lived according to the laws of nature, i.e. the laws of our creator. It has been proposed that since then we have been evolving toward a stage where we will use our free will to once again live according to the laws of our creator, as communicated to us by God's messengers. As such this is a very exciting time for humanity, the culmination of thousands of years of evolution.

It seems obvious to say that our lives should be lived in the context of conscious knowledge of our purpose. This realization, besides being logical, is the hallmark of a mature individual and a mature society. Lack of knowledge of purpose reduces our lives to a series of seemingly random events, and results in an unstable society, which we can see today. Knowledge of the purpose of any created thing resides with its creator. We have made a case for the existence of a creator, and proposed that knowledge of purpose has been communicated to us via religion, which is renewed every thousand years or so. We summarize as follows:

- Human purpose is bound up with the development of our spiritual nature - with our ability to conform with the will of God, like every other created thing
- Our (hopefully fully developed) spirit is all we take with us to the next life, so it makes sense to work on its development now
- We need to exercise our free will to investigate the purpose of our lives, something that has not been common in the past
- The events of our lives provide opportunities for this development, and complement our individual efforts
- Happiness is a by-product of this journey

Over the course of your life you accumulate knowledge. Imagine that you place each new piece of knowledge in a file folder. The ideas in this book are intended to help you construct a file *cabinet*, i.e. a structure or framework for organizing your understandings. I hope that at a minimum the thoughts and the rather simple conclusions of this book give you the courage to actively pursue (or continue to pursue) your own thoughts on this subject. If it is like my own experience, it will be a humbling and ongoing process. You never "arrive", you just agree to take the journey - but it is a rewarding journey.

APPENDIX 1 - Guidance from religion concerning service

These words of the founders of great religions demonstrate the essential oneness of religion. Other divine teachings also do this (e.g. every religion has a statement equivalent to the Golden Rule).

Hinduism (Krishna)

- "At the beginning of time I declared two paths for the pure heart: the contemplative path of spiritual wisdom, and the active path of selfless service."
- "At the beginning, mankind and the obligation of selfless service were created together. 'Through selfless service, you will always be fruitful and find the fulfilment of your desires': this is the promise of the Creator."
- "Strive constantly to serve the welfare of the world; by devotion to selfless work one attains the supreme goal of life. Do your work with the welfare of others always in mind."

Christianity (Jesus Christ)

- "For you were called to freedom, brothers. Only do not use your freedom as an opportunity for the flesh, but through love serve one another."
- "Even as the Son of Man came not to be served but to serve."

- "And he sat down and called the twelve. And he said to them, 'If anyone would be first, he must be last of all and servant of all.'"

Islam (Muhammad)

- "And worship Allah and associate naught with Him and show kindness to parents, and to kindred, and orphans, and the needy, and to the neighbor that is a kinsman and the neighbor that is a stranger, and the companion by your side, and the wayfarer... Surely, Allah loves not the proud and the boastful."
- "...you have been raised to serve others; you enjoin what is good and forbid evil and believe in Allah."
- "Surely Allah enjoins the doing of justice and the doing of good (for others)."

Bahá'í Faith (Bahá'u'lláh)

- "The Great Being saith: Blessed and happy is he that ariseth to promote the best interests of the peoples and kindreds of the earth."
- "It is not for him to pride himself who loveth his own country, but rather for him who loveth the whole world. The earth is but one country, and mankind its citizens."
- "That one indeed is a man who, today, dedicateth himself to the service of the entire human race."

APPENDIX 2 - The Will of God

Introduction

The maturity of the human race will be marked by human beings using their free will to align themselves with the will of God, both individually and collectively. We are told that "Whatsoever (we wish) to do must be in harmony with the good pleasure of God. (We) must observe and see what is the will of God and act accordingly."[1] We are also told that communities and institutions should strive to align themselves with the will of God.[2] This is a central principle of sustainable development.

So how do we know what the will of God is? The focus of this paper is to investigate this question. We will first explore how God's will is made manifest in the physical world, and then how it is made manifest to the world of humanity. In the process we will hopefully discover some of the significances and implications of our conscious efforts to help fulfill Christ's prayer that "Thy (God's) will be done on earth as it is in heaven."

God's Will for the Physical World

Nature is the material world. We notice that nature operates according to the will of God. We are told that "Nature is God's Will and is its expression in and

---

[1] Abdu'l-Bahá, *The Promulgation of Universal Peace*, p.236

[2] Universal House of Justice, January 9, 2001, letter to the Conference of the Continental Boards of Counselors

through the contingent world. It is a dispensation of Providence ordained by the Ordainer, the All-Wise. Were anyone to affirm that it is the Will of God as manifested in the world of being, no one should question this assertion."[3] We could express the relationship between God and the physical world as shown in Figure 1.

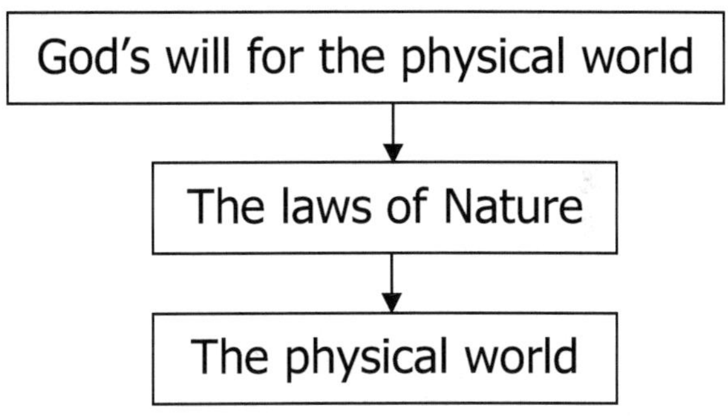

Figure 1 - the relationship between God and the physical world (first attempt)

The natural world has no option but to operate according to the will of God, as it has no free will. It is "hardwired" to behave as it does, and it cannot deviate from the laws of nature. For example, the bee is created to make its hive only in the form of a hexagon; it cannot choose to build it in a different form.

Bahá'u'lláh tells us that God's creation is perfect. "So perfect and comprehensive is His creation that no mind

[3] Bahá'u'lláh, *Tablets of Bahá'u'lláh Revealed after the Kitáb-i-Aqdas*, p.142

nor heart, however keen or pure, can ever grasp the nature of the most insignificant of His creatures."[4] However, it turns out that nature is imperfect. "Nature is the material world. When we look upon it, we see that it is dark and imperfect. For instance, if we allow a piece of land to remain in its natural condition, we will find it covered with thorns and thistles; useless weeds and wild vegetation will flourish upon it, and it will become like a jungle. The trees will be fruitless, lacking beauty and symmetry; wild animals, noxious insects and reptiles will abound in its dark recesses. This is the incompleteness and imperfection of the world of nature."[5]

If nature is God's will and nature is imperfect, surely we cannot be saying that God's will is imperfect! One way of resolving these two statements is to consider that maybe nature is not the sole expression of God's will for the physical world. As suggested in Figure 2, humanity also influences the physical world, and should do so according to the will of God. The forces of nature alone will not result in a perfect physical world. It is God's will that man, along with the forces of Nature, play a part in shaping the physical world.

Similarly we can resolve the two statements that God's creation is perfect and that nature is imperfect when we realize that there is more to God's creation than nature. The added ingredient is humanity. We are told that

---

[4] Bahá'u'lláh, *Tablets of Bahá'u'lláh Revealed after the Kitáb-i-Aqdas*, p.62

[5] Abdu'l-Bahá, *The Promulgation of Universal Peace*, p.308

"...it (nature) is nevertheless, imperfect because it has need of intelligence and education"[6], and that is our role.

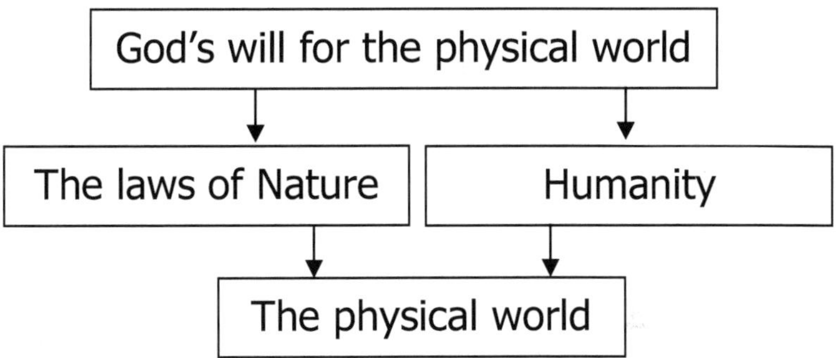

Figure 2 - the relationship between God and the physical world (second attempt)

Humanity undoubtedly has an influence on the physical world. As we exercise our free will, we may or may not act in accordance with the will of the Creator in our treatment of the physical world. Clearly it is suffering under our stewardship at the present time. There is only one component of creation that is not operating according to the will of God, and that is us.

Up until now humanity has had limited effect upon the planet, as the human population was relatively small and technological progress limited. We now need to appreciate the complexities of the natural world and our interactions with it in order play our part in the creation of God's kingdom on earth in the physical sense. This of course will assist us in our never-ending efforts to

[6] ibid, p.329

know God, in the same way that intimate knowledge of the painting helps us to know and appreciate the painter. We are told "Out of the wastes of nothingness, with the clay of My command I made thee to appear, and have ordained for thy training every atom in existence and the essence of all created things."[7]

For us the physical world is an incubator or womb. It is a place where God trains us in preparation for the next life. So we are "born" from this life - from the Earth, from the physical world - into the next. This may well be one of the reasons why many cultures have traditionally personified nature as being female (e.g. Mother Earth, Mother Nature).

We are told that "religion is the revelation of the will of God".[8] If humanity chooses to act according to the teachings of religion, then the full benefit of God's will is received by the physical world, as suggested in Figure 2. In this way physical creation, which is potentially perfect, can become actually perfect. It is God's will that humanity work along with the laws of nature to shape and perfect the physical world. We are charged with creating a sustainable society that is in line with the will of God.

This leads us to the second part of the paper - a discussion of how God's will is made manifest to the world of humanity.

---

[7] Bahá'u'lláh, Persian *Hidden Words*

[8] Abdu'l-Bahá, *The Promulgation of Universal Peace*, p.315

God's Will for Humanity

Previous quotations make it clear that God's will for humanity is embodied in the teachings of religion. This would suggest the model shown in Figure 3 below for how God's will is revealed to us. We are told that "the will of God will become the will of man, and the earth a veritable habitation of angels."[9] It is encouraging to realize that we will ultimately succeed in aligning ourselves with His will to a high degree.

Humanity has a Covenant with its Creator, and this is succinctly stated as follows: "The first duty prescribed by God for His servants is the recognition of Him Who is the Dayspring of His Revelation and the Fountain of His laws, Who representeth the Godhead in both the Kingdom of His Cause and the world of creation. Whoso achieveth this duty hath attained unto all good; and whoso is deprived thereof hath gone astray, though he be the author of every righteous deed. It behoveth every one who reacheth this most sublime station, this summit of transcendent glory, to observe every ordinance of Him Who is the Desire of the world. These twin duties are inseparable. Neither is acceptable without the other. Thus hath it been decreed by Him Who is the Source of Divine inspiration."[10]

Therefore it is God's will that we should a) use our free will to recognize God's Manifestation, and then b) do what He says. God's part of this Covenant is to assist us

---

[9] ibid, p.320

[10] Bahá'u'lláh, *The Kitáb-i-Aqdas*, p.19

to lead happy and fulfilling lives - to achieve our potential as human beings. "The Manifestations have the particular function of revealing the Will of God to humanity."[11]

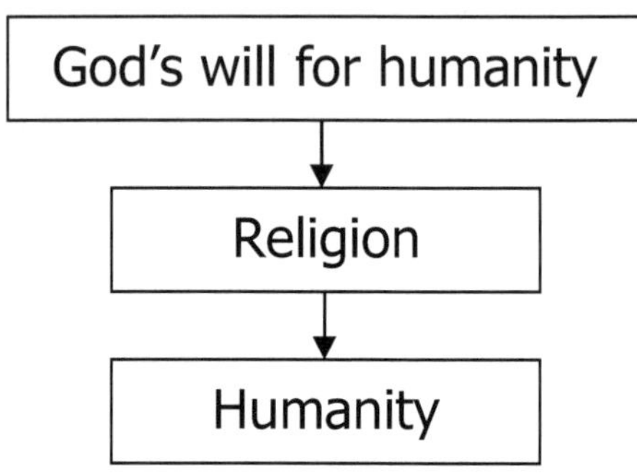

Figure 3 - the relationship between God and humanity (first attempt)

Religion, as revealed by God's Manifestations, provides the primary indication of God's will. However there are also other ways in which God's will becomes known to us. For example, we are told "The question of [divine] guidance is a very subtle one. We cannot be positive that an impulse or a dream is guidance. We can seek, through earnest prayer and longing, sincerely to do God's will, His guidance. We... cannot be sure that doing these things we are still making no mistakes and are perfectly guided. These things help us not to make so many mistakes and to receive more directly the guidance God seeks to give us."[12]

---

[11] Letters of The Universal House of Justice, 1992 Feb 23, Ancient Goddess Religions

[12] Shoghi Effendi, Directives from the Guardian, p.35

Figure 4 includes that added component suggested in the quotation. By "inspiration" is meant those insights we gain through individual prayer, meditation, intuition and dreams. This inspiration may or may not represent the will of God, and the guidance of the revealed Word of God is preferable if it is available. Nonetheless inspiration is a mechanism through which we can know God's will.

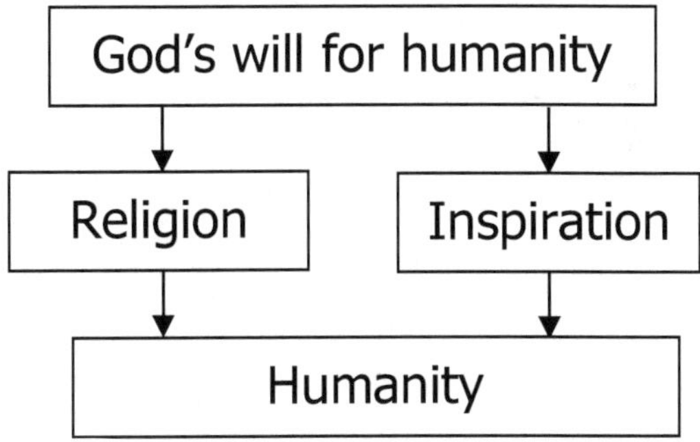

Figure 4 - the relationship between God and humanity (second attempt)

It is interesting to note that we are not completely free to do as we please in this life. "...Some things are subject to the free will of man, such as justice, equity, tyranny and injustice, in other words, good and evil actions; it is evident and clear that these actions are, for the most part, left to the will of man. But there are certain things to which man is forced and compelled, such as sleep, death, sickness, decline of power, injuries and misfortunes; these are not subject to the will of man, and he is not responsible for them, for he is compelled to endure them. But in the choice of good and bad actions he is free, and he commits them according to his own will."[13]

It is clear that some of our "injuries and misfortunes" represent the will of God. We are told "My (God's) calamity is My providence, outwardly it is fire and vengeance, but inwardly it is light and mercy."[14] God, as his part of the Covenant, takes every event of our lives and makes it a means for our spiritual advancement. "Life afflicts us with very severe trials sometimes, but we must always remember that when we accept patiently the will of God He compensates us in other ways. With faith and love we must be patient, and He will surely reward us."[15] Therefore the will of God can be made known to us through "life". We are told "Ask not of Me (God) that which We desire not for thee, then be content with what We have ordained for thy sake, for this is that which profiteth thee, if therewith thou dost content thyself."[16] Of course this applies to both good and bad life experiences.

It is also suggested in the Writings that God's will can be made known to us through consultation. "We are often told by the Master that under such circumstances we should consult our friends... and seek their advice. It would be nice if you should follow that advice and

---

[13] Abdu'l-Bahá, *Some Answered Questions*, p.248

[14] Bahá'u'lláh, Arabic *Hidden Words*

[15] Shoghi Effendi, *Lights of Guidance*, p.603

[16] Bahá'u'lláh, Arabic *Hidden Words*

take some of the friends into your confidence. Maybe God's will is best attained through consultation."[17]

Taking the two most recent points, we can now augment our model of how God's will becomes known to humanity as shown in Figure 5.

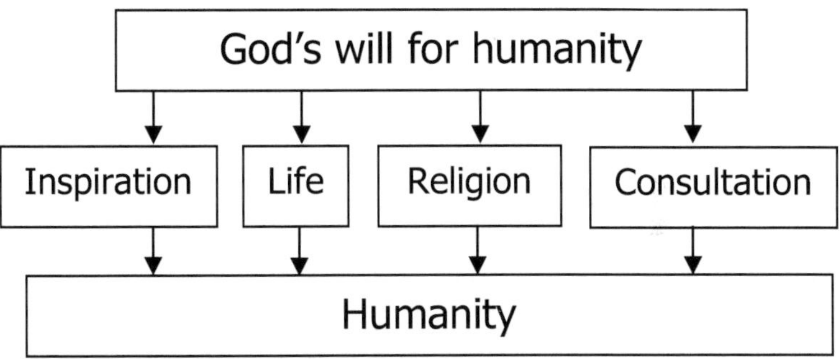

Figure 5 - the relationship between God and humanity (third attempt)

Therefore we can seek God's will for us in religion, through inspiration, consultation and in our interpretation of the affairs of our lives. It is important to stress that religion is the primary source for authoritative knowledge of the will of God.

Many of the affairs of our lives do not represent the will of God. This becomes clear when one considers that every human being has free will, and that human beings obviously impact other human lives. We are told "...but in the choice of good and bad actions he is free, and he

[17] Written on behalf of Shoghi Effendi, *The Compilation of Compilations* vol. I, p.103

commits them according to his own will." For example if a bomb is detonated during rush hour in a city causing death and destruction, this is not God's will. It is the misdirected exercising of human free will. Of course God has the knowledge that this event is going to happen, but that doesn't mean He willed it to happen. As 'Abdu'l-Bahá explains "This knowledge and these prophecies were not the cause of the occurrences. For example, tonight everyone knows that after seven hours the sun will rise, but this general foreknowledge does not cause the rising and appearance of the sun."[18]

In the opinion of the author, when other human beings impact our lives by exercising their free will (which is often), God then takes our lives and guides us to learn from these events. But human free will is part of creation, and God generally doesn't prevent us from misbehaving. We can often see God's wisdom in the affairs of our lives, but some of that guidance is His reaction to what we or other human beings have caused to occur. In this way God's loving presence exists in the affairs of every human being on a daily basis.

> "God has created His servants in order that they may love and associate with each other. He has revealed the glorious splendor of His sun of love in the world of humanity. The cause of the creation of the phenomenal world is love. All the Prophets have promulgated the law of love. Man has opposed the will of God and acted in opposition to the plan of God. Therefore, from the beginning of history to the

---

[18] Abdu'l-Bahá, *Some Answered Questions*, p.138

present time the world of humanity has had no lasting rest; warfare and strife have continuously prevailed, and hearts have manifested hatred toward each other."[19]

The will of God is an expression of God's love for humanity. "... religion must be the mainspring and source of love in the world, for religion is the revelation of the will of God, the divine fundamental of which is love."[20]

Conclusion

"To attain the pleasure of God is the most important thing. Thank God thou art content with the will of God and art attached in heart to His divine wishes; and as thou art thus, all thy desires will be granted thee."[21] When conforming ourselves to the will of God, naturally our desires are granted - we are working in harmony with creation.

The physical world comes to be in accordance with the will of God through both the laws of nature and the actions of human beings. Humanity comes to be in accordance with the will of God through doing their part in obeying God's Covenant. This requires active investigation and implementation of God's teachings, as well as the discerning of God's will through consultation, personal inspiration and in the events of their lives.

---

[19] Abdu'l-Bahá, *The Promulgation of Universal Peace*, p.297

[20] ibid, p.315

[21] Abdu'l-Bahá, *Tablets of Abdu'l-Bahá v2*, p.456

We can be encouraged by knowing that God's Kingdom on earth will indeed be established in due course. Our humble efforts will be rewarded when we put them in line with the will of God.

> "Let us pray to God that the breath of the Holy Spirit may again give hope and refreshment to the people, awakening in them a desire to do the Will of God. May heart and soul be vivified in every man: so will they all rejoice in a new birth. Then shall humanity put on a new garment in the radiance of the love of God, and it shall be the dawn of a new creation! Then will the Mercy of the Most Merciful be showered upon all mankind and they will arise to a new life."[22]

[22] Abdu'l-Bahá, *Paris Talks*, p.34

APPENDIX 3 - Science and Religion

Functions of Religion and Science

We live in a womb-world. It is our duty in this life to recognize God's messenger and then to try to do all that He says.[23] This results in our soul developing those attributes of God that are latent within us (patience, compassion, etc.) to a greater or lesser degree, depending on our efforts and opportunities. At the end of this process our soul is born into the next life.

Therefore it is the function of society to strive to create the optimum conditions in our collective womb for the spiritual development of every human being. This is a complex task, and one that is not occupying the minds of the leaders of society at present. But it will in due course, as we mature as a race.

Religion has a direct effect on our spiritual development. We are told that "Religion, moreover, is not a series of beliefs, a set of customs; *religion is the teachings of the Lord God*, teachings which constitute the very life of humankind, which urge high thoughts upon the mind, refine the character, and lay the groundwork for man's everlasting honour."[24]

So the function of religion is to make us better people, while it is the function of science to facilitate material

---

[23] Bahá'u'lláh, *Kitáb-i-Aqdas*, first paragraph

[24] 'Abdu'l-Bahá, *Selections from the Writings of Abdu'l-Bahá*, p.52, emphasis added

development, which in turn assists the spiritual development of humankind. In other words, science serves religion.

The Harmony of Religion and Science

Dictionary definitions of religion and science are as follows:

- Religion - 1) the belief in and worship of a superhuman controlling power, especially a personal God or gods 2) a particular system of faith and worship[25]
- Science - 1) the intellectual and practical activity encompassing the systematic study of the structure and behaviour of the physical and natural world through observation and experiment, and 2) a systematically organized body of knowledge on any subject[26]

A person I admire once proposed that "religion is what came out of the mouth of Christ" (i.e. God's messenger). If we use that definition, then religion is not something that is up for debate, rather it is something that we need to strive to understand and implement.

"Weigh not the Book of God with such standards and sciences as are current amongst you, for the Book itself is the unerring Balance established amongst men. In

---

[25] *The Concise Oxford Dictionary*, 10th Edition
[26] ibid

this most perfect Balance whatsoever the peoples and kindreds of the earth possess must be weighed, while the measure of its weight should be tested according to its own standard, did ye but know it."[27]

Therefore if religion and science seem to disagree, either our science is incorrect or we are not understanding God's Teachings, or both. For example if science proves the value of red wine in extending human life, and religion forbids red wine, we don't conclude that religion is wrong. We might conclude that there is possibly something of value in red wine, and proceed to investigate how to extract that value without taking the wine. We will be continually faced with seeming contradictions such as this between religion and science, contradictions which will only be understood over time. This state of ambiguity is to be expected.

"With regard to the harmony of science and religion, the Writings... make abundantly clear that the task of humanity... is to create a global civilization which embodies both the spiritual and material dimensions of existence. The nature and scope of such a civilization are still beyond anything the present generation can conceive. The prosecution of this vast enterprise will depend on a progressive interaction between the truths and principles of religion and the discoveries and insights of scientific inquiry. This entails living with

---

[27] Bahá'u'lláh, Kitáb-i-Aqdas, p.56

ambiguities as a natural and inescapable feature of the process of exploring reality."[28]

Understanding that we don't understand very much relative to what can be known is a mark of maturity. The true scientist is humble, and will be comfortable when confronted with his or her own ignorance, realizing that this is a normal human condition. Consider this: at the present time a vast majority of human beings are not realizing their potential and yet knowledge is advancing at an unprecedented rate. In the future Golden Age, a majority of human beings will realize their potential, and knowledge will increase maybe 100 times faster than now. Human knowledge will truly be vast. Yet there will always be something new to be known. Since the universe if infinite (infinitely large, infinitely small, infinitely complex) it follows there are an infinity of things to be known. Clearly we presently know almost nothing.

A mathematical way of considering our ignorance is to observe that any number divided by infinity is zero, therefore what we know is nothing relative to what there is to be known. If X is what we know, then we see that, according to the laws of mathematics, X divided by infinity is zero. From that perspective it is clear we know nothing.

"In each drop of water are hidden oceans of meaning, and in each mote is concealed a whole universe of

---

[28] 19 May 1995, written on behalf of the Universal House of Justice to an individual believer, emphasis added

significances, reaching far beyond the ken of the most learned scientist. The chemist and physicist pursuing their researches into the nature of matter have passed from masses to molecules, from molecules to atoms, from atoms to electrons and ether, but at every step the difficulties of the research increase till the most profound intellect can penetrate no farther....

Flower in the crannied wall,
I pluck you out of the crannies.
I hold you here, root and all, in my hand,
Little flower -- but if I could understand
What you are, root and all, and all in all,
I should know what God and man is."[29]

Science and the Scientific Method

"The Revelation proclaimed by Bahá'u'lláh, His followers believe, is divine in origin, all embracing in scope, broad in its outlook, scientific in its method, humanitarian in its principles and dynamic in the influence it exerts on the hearts and minds of men."[30]

The Bahá'í Faith is the first revealed religion since the advent of the scientific method. Let us say that formal experimental science began with Galileo (1564-1642). We see that this is well after the advent of Islam (Muhammad passed away in 632AD). We note that the

---

[29] Tennyson, quoted by Dr J.E. Esslemont, *Bahá'u'lláh and the New Era,* p.202

[30] Shoghi Effendi, Extracts from the US Bahá'í News No. 85 - July 1934

word "science" does not appear in the Qur'an (or the Bible, for that matter). Therefore we cannot expect any other traditional religion to appear "scientific in its method", since the human race didn't really think this way until recently.

The scientific method can be illustrated as shown in Figure 1. There are essentially two steps to the scientific method – theorizing and testing. A theory is thought of and then the theory is tested. If it is fully satisfactory then no modification is needed, however it is continually re-tested in the light of new knowledge. If the theory eventually proves to be incorrect or needs modification, then the cycle starts again.

In broad terms (though by no means exclusively), the theorizing part is spiritual and the testing part is intellectual. When we seek to gain new insights in any area, we might first pray for assistance. We then might meditate upon a potential theory based on our present knowledge and being alert to the promptings of our mind and heart. The moment when a new idea hits us is often quite magical, and need not occur when we are particularly addressing our mind to the issue. For example a professor friend of mine had been considering the reasons for the configuration of the earth's magnetic field without much success, and then one night when he was lying awake in bed, almost delirious from the flu (and not particularly thinking about the issue) he had a "eureka moment" when an important new theory came to him.

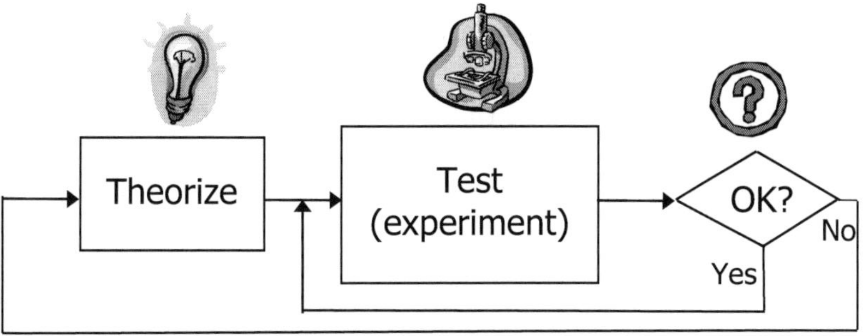

Figure 1 - the Scientific Method

The mathematician George Boole said "Geometric induction is essentially a process of prayer -- an appeal from the finite mind to the Infinite for light on finite concerns."[31] The statement could be applied to other arts and sciences.

The "test" part of the scientific method requires testing your idea against known facts. You may have to design a test, the result of which will hopefully support your theory. The testing process is greatly facilitated by knowledge. For example if you are researching cancer, you should obviously have familiarity with previous research in the area. If you are investigating meditation, it helps to be familiar the writings of various philosophers and religions against which you test your ideas. Without this knowledge the validity of your idea is less likely to be correct since it has not been adequately tested.

---

[31] Boole, quoted in Dr J.E. Esslemont, *Bahá'u'lláh and the New Era*, p. 197

We can also test theories with our heart. Does it "feel right"? What does your intuition tell you? Of course this is a "softer" test, and the results of the test cannot be binding on anyone else, but you can test your theories against your head and your heart. For example, "After the Lord Christ suffered, the disciples wept, and gave way to their grief. They thought that their hopes were shattered, and that the Cause was utterly lost, till Mary Magdalene came to them and strengthened them saying: 'Do you mourn the body of Our Lord or His Spirit? If you mourn His Spirit, you are mistaken, for Jesus lives! His Spirit will never leave us!' Thus through her wisdom and encouragement the Cause of Christ was upheld for all the days to come. Her intuition enabled her to grasp the spiritual fact."

Investigation of Truth

From the above we see that we can use a systematic methodology to investigate truth of any sort. Based on the dictionary definition of science above, an important element of the scientific investigation of truth is that it be systematic.

Many people consider themselves "scientific" in their rejection of spiritual matters. They refuse to believe what they cannot see (what about radio waves?), and consider faith irrational (every time we use a map it is an act of faith in the cartographer). They might (illogically) believe in the existence of a creation without a Creator. This is partly due to the discrediting of religion by ignorant leaders of religion who insist on clinging to irrational interpretations and dogma from the past which have little or no basis in the Word of God.

"The truth is no dead thing, to be placed in a museum when found -- to be labeled, classified, catalogued, exhibited and left there, dry and sterile. It is something vital which must take root in men's hearts and bear fruit in their lives ere they reap the full reward of their search."[32] The investigation of truth is for everyone, in every facet of human life.

We live in a technological age, where until recently many felt that technology could solve all of society's problems. Instead, problems are multiplying as the "old world order" is rolled up. This is sometimes seen, consciously or subconsciously, as a failure of science. Therefore, to some extent, at the present time both science and religion are discredited. In fact science has performed well. Science is necessary but simply insufficient on its own to bring about a peaceful global society.

Conclusion

Truth is truth, and all truth can and should be considered with our God-given intellect. The investigation of truth is always rewarded. The process for the systematic investigation of truth is not confined to any field of knowledge. Come up with your theories, meditate upon your ideas using your head and your heart, and test them in light of existing known truths.

---

[32] Dr J.E. Esslemont, *Bahá'u'lláh and the New Era*, p.10

The systematic discovery and implementation of spiritual and scientific truth is the key to creating God's kingdom on earth.

"Put all your beliefs into harmony with science; there can be no opposition, for truth is one. When religion, shorn of its superstitions, traditions, and unintelligent dogmas, shows its conformity with science, then will there be a great unifying, cleansing force in the world which will sweep before it all wars, disagreements, discords and struggles -- and then will mankind be united in the power of the Love of God."

About the Author

Lawrence Staudt is from the north-eastern United States. He grew up in New Jersey and Connecticut. Early in his engineering career he became aware of the unsustainable nature of present day society, and decided to do something about it. He left his conventional engineering job to pursue renewable energy engineering, and eventually became engineering manager of a Vermont wind energy company.

He and his wife Dawn and their children moved to Ireland in 1985, where he continued his efforts in sustainable energy. He eventually lectured in the subject at Dundalk Institute of Technology, where he headed a research center. Now retired, he has kept active in the energy area, serving at the Bahá'í World Center in Haifa, Israel, primarily in the area of energy conservation.

He has also written a number of children's books on social/environmental themes, as well as anecdotes from his childhood growing up in America in the 50s and 60s. He has been interested in purpose and meaning in life from a young age, and this book is the result of his years of wondering about such things.

Printed in Poland
by Amazon Fulfillment
Poland Sp. z o.o., Wrocław